THE PRICE OF FREEDOM

THE PRICE OF FREEDOM

COURAGE IN THE SHADOW OF THE BERLIN WALL

VOLKER G. HEINZ

AMBERLEY

To my wife and my children, with thanks for their encouragement, help, and patience.

I am also grateful to Regina Carstensen and Clara Polley for their advice and help when writing the German edition of this book.

My thanks also go to Sir Konrad Schiemann for kindly providing the foreword to this work.

'Courage is rightly considered the foremost of the virtues, for upon it all others depend.'

Winston Churchill

This English edition translated by David Antal
in cooperation with the author and
his wife Sandra Tancibudek-Heinz

First published 2019

Amberley Publishing
The Hill, Stroud
Gloucestershire, GL5 4EP

www.amberley-books.com

The names of some of the persons in this book
have been changed to protect their privacy.
The names of persons in public life are
unchanged.

Original edition published by Rowohlt
Taschenbuch Verlag, Reinbeck bei Hamburg,
September 2016

ISBN 978 1 4456 9233 3 (paperback)
ISBN 978 1 4456 9234 0 (ebook)

British Library Cataloguing in Publication Data.
A catalogue record for this book is available
from the British Library.

Typesetting by Aura Technology and Software
Services, India. Printed in the UK.

CONTENTS

VOLKER G. HEINZ was born in Kassel in central Germany in 1943 during the Allied bombing campaign which destroyed about 90 per cent of that city. He attended school as a classical scholar in Bavaria and Westphalia. After short spells as a student of mechanical engineering, economics and philosophy, he studied German law in Heidelberg, Berlin and Bonn, and English law at the City University in London. He is a multilingual business lawyer, licensed to practise both in Germany and England and Wales as Rechtsanwalt/Barrister-at-Law and Notar/Scrivener Notary.

He has co-authored and co-edited a number of text books on German commercial and company law. He also wrote the first German book on English Limited companies. For many years he chaired Berlin's largest tenants' associations, working hard to improve and protect the rights of their members, not least through his regular TV and radio appearances.

In 2001 he established the Anglo-German Foundation 'Temple Gift', a gesture both of thanks to his Inn of Court and of reconciliation between former World War enemies. The foundation established a scholarship for young barristers working in Germany and presented four stone benches and an organ to Temple Church. The organ replaces an earlier instrument much played by Händel, which was destroyed by bombing in 1940.

FOREWORD

We are led by the author of this exciting autobiographical sketch into the Cold War world of the 1960s. This world's undisputed centre was Berlin, divided by a wall, separating families, friends, opposite political systems and ideas. It also was the city where spies from many countries thrived, while people in East Berlin tried to penetrate the wall with the help of West Berlin-based *Fluchthelfer* (escape helpers), mostly youngsters daring to help Easterners to escape. Few people now living had any experience of this world, of which not much is widely known.

In 1945, at the end of the Second World War, the victorious Soviets, Americans, British and French had rearranged the map of Europe leaving Germany a much smaller country. They divided that smaller Germany into four zones of occupation. In 1949 the Soviets created out of their zone the German Democratic Republic (GDR), which was run by their omnipotent communist party. The remaining British, American and French zones became The German Federal Republic (FRG), also known as West Germany. Berlin, the former capital of Germany, situated in the middle of the Soviet zone, was also divided into four zones. All Allies had free access to each other's zones, whereas the population could only travel with express permission. The Eastern Soviet zone of Berlin became the GDR's capital, Bonn the capital of West Germany. Bonn regarded West Berlin as part of its political system against vehement opposition from the Soviet Union and its vassal state GDR, and for many years refused formally to acknowledge the legitimacy of the GDR, demanding instead the reunification of both Germanys.

By the 1960s the FRG was an economic success and as democratic as it is now. The GDR was far less successful and distinctly less free, so many in the GDR wanted to escape to the West. This was forbidden under GDR law, which did not want to lose part of its population. It found it humiliating that many wanted to escape from what was officially named a 'workers' and farmers' paradise'. Anyone trying to leave the GDR without permission was arrested or shot. Many, many were.

Nevertheless, millions of East Germans did escape to the West, which prompted the GDR to build the Berlin wall between its three Western zones and its Eastern zone in August 1961. Plenty of watch towers, guard dogs, barbed wire and firearms made it near impossible to cross the wall. The whole of the western border of the GDR was similarly fortified. Any attempt to cross the border put one's life in immediate danger.

It was in this world that Volker Heinz, a West German law student, now an English barrister and notary as well as a practising German lawyer, moved to Berlin. Observing on a daily basis the cruelty of the wall, suddenly separating friends and loved ones, he decided to help GDR citizens escape into freedom. This book is a gripping tale of how he, jointly with others, succeeded in smuggling more than 60 people through the wall into West Berlin. The excitement that gripped him in turn grips the reader. Heinz has a good command of language and keeps the reader on tenterhooks. One flies from page to page in order to see what happens next. Eventually the East German authorities observed and in due course caught him. The 23-year-old found himself in prison cells where he was repeatedly interrogated and subjected to a series of mistreatments for the sole reason of helping others escape from East to West Berlin.

But this book is much more than a thriller. Heinz recounts details of the system of human trafficking which was jointly instituted by the GDR and the FRG to secure the release of prisoners. Between 1963 and 1989, some 34.000 political prisoners were released through this mechanism, fuelled by transfers of money and goods to the GDR worth some 3 billion Deutschmarks. Occasionally the FRG released spies whom they had captured in return for prisoners held by the GDR. Heinz describes this secret mechanism, and how the German Protestant Church knowingly acted as facilitator.

But the book is about more than escapes, imprisonment and prisoner swaps. Heinz also offers glimpses of the student fraternities in the FRG and West Berlin. Indeed, Heinz owed his eventual release in part to one member of his own Heidelberg fraternity, Hans Martin Schleyer, who was later murdered by the Baader Meinhof gang.

Heinz is now in his seventies. His book contains the generous reflections of an older man on the wild enthusiasm of his youth, on the taking of risks for a good cause, on a fraught relationship with his father, on the persons who influenced his decision to engage in this dangerous work, and on those who had cooperated with the GDR authorities at his expense. In Germany, *Zivilcourage* (civic courage), the courage of the civilian as opposed to the military, is greatly valued. Reading stories of those who resisted dictatorship, I am always humbled by the fact that I have never been required to show it. Others, including the author of this book, have, and I have found reading about his adventures irresistible.

Sir Konrad Schiemann PC

(Sir Konrad Schiemann was born in Berlin in 1937. He was orphaned during the war and came to England in 1946. He attended King Edward's School in Birmingham and was commissioned into the Lancashire Fusiliers, serving in Cyprus. He holds a Master of Arts and Bachelor of Laws from Cambridge University and is an Honorary Fellow of Pembroke College, Cambridge. He practised as a barrister from 1964, became a Queen's Counsel in 1980, a High Court Judge in 1986 and a Lord Justice of Appeal in 1995. He is a bencher of the Inner Temple and was a judge of the Court of Justice of the European Union between 2004 and 2012.)

PROLOGUE

The sky over East Berlin was darkening. It was May 1966. Exhausted, I wiped the sweat from my forehead. It had been a long, hard day. Instead of going to the preparatory course for my law exams, I had driven in the early morning my pale blue Volkswagen from Bonn to Cologne-Wahn airport and had flown from there to Tempelhof airport in West Berlin to receive my instructions. I entered East Berlin through the border checkpoint at Heinrich Heine Strasse. From there I took the rapid transit railway, the S-Bahn, out to Köpenick and walked the rest of the way. I lingered for a moment in front of the Rittersberger family home, gathering myself, then took a deep breath and rang the bell. Dr Max Rittersberger opened the door and let me in. He shook my hand, his face grave. He looked as though he had been expecting me for a long time.

A slender man of medium height, whose brown hair betrayed the first hints of grey, he led me into the living room where his wife looked at me as expectantly as his three adolescent children, Stefan, Maximilian, and Katharina. The youngest child, a little girl of about two years of age, was asleep in the living room. I sat down, gratefully accepting a cup of tea. We spoke about the procedure for the escape that was to take place that very evening; the first one, for the three older children. The parents were to follow with their younger daughter in a second operation the next day. Never before had I met would-be escapees at their home. What was happening was an absolute exception. Normally, Wolfgang's couriers planned the details and then instructed the persons who wanted to escape. But today this was my job. I sat there explaining to the family how they were supposed to cross Berlin's border between the two Germanys by hiding in the boot of a car.

A few hours later I was standing in the middle of Alexanderplatz. Even from a distance I could see the three siblings huddled anxiously at the foot of the television tower. Hopefully they had not come to the attention of East Germany's state security police, the Stasi; this was certainly not my idea of looking inconspicuous. They were supposed to be eating ice cream and mingling with the crowd - that crowd was the reason we had chosen Alexanderplatz to meet.

'Is there a department store nearby?' I asked, our agreed code to start the conversation.

The three nodded and replied as arranged: 'On the other side of the tram stop. We'll show you if you'd like.'

I nodded likewise. The four of us set off. We were not heading for the store but the tram. We boarded a tram that I had selected earlier, switched to another line, and continued to one of the last stops east. From there we walked towards Marzahn-Hellersdorf, a rural area further east of the city. The prefab high-rise settlement that was later to be built here was, at best, still only in the planning stage. We remained silent most of the way. The three young people barely said a word. I tried repeatedly to smile and cheer things up a little, being in need of some cheering up myself.

I no longer knew how many people I had brought over the border. It was a strenuous job that had over time lost some of its once electrifying thrill. Each time I sensed the fear of the others almost physically, having to bear it along with my own while compensating for it and dispelling it at the same time. Often enough I had experienced how unpredictably and heedlessly the fugitives behaved. From one time to the next it was becoming harder for me. For I had to act like master of the situation and, above all, I had to come up with the goods: their long-sought freedom. These people were relying on me. And I knew that what I was doing here was meaningful. I was also determined to continue helping, convinced that it was the right thing to do. But it demanded a lot of self-discipline. I was not paid for my help, and to me it was very important that it stayed that way. Recently I had learned that a great deal of money was involved in these escapes.

Although I didn't like to admit it, my double life was weighing more and more heavily on me. I constantly had to spin a web of lies to deceive my family and friends. No one beyond the close circle of the escape helpers knew what I was doing, except for one person: Hanns Martin Schleyer, my fraternity brother. I had confided in him a short while ago. It was for him that I was organising this escape. The three young people accompanying me belonged to an East Berlin physician's family who meant a lot to Schleyer. Their mother was the sister of another fraternity brother. In a fraternity, you help each other out.

Hardly anyone was out and about in this part of Marzahn. The girl and the two boys followed me up a narrow lane. There was no oncoming traffic, and no car passed us. Fields of tall grain soon to be harvested lined both sides of the path, shielding us from prying eyes. My thoughts were revolving around the next step. Hopefully it would all go well; hopefully the Syrian would be there. What if he'd had a flat tyre or been held up by something else? What would I do with this trio then? I had to be back in the West by midnight at the latest. It would be illegal for me to stay longer than that. I tried to calm down, reminding myself that the family did live here in East Berlin. At a pinch the three could just go back home as though nothing had happened.

Dusk had long since fallen. The darker it grew, the safer I felt. At the next crossing we turned right. If everything had gone smoothly, that is where Kamal Hamdi would be waiting to drive slowly towards us. A first glance around the corner made me breathe a sigh of relief – the white Mercedes was easily recognisable. When the Syrian saw me, he flashed his lights. I drew a small torch from the pocket of my jacket and signalled the Mercedes that all was well. Then everything went very quickly. I pushed the three teenagers towards the car's boot and opened it.

'Get in,' I whispered whilst looking around feverishly. Hopefully no other car was approaching at that moment. I felt fresh beads of sweat forming on my forehead, although the temperature was nowhere near as high as it had been on Alexanderplatz.

They lay down one behind the other like spoons, as though they had practised. I cast a final glance at their pale, fear-ridden faces. Hopefully they will get through OK, I thought to myself. 'Good luck,' I said and then shut the boot. I took a deep breath. The Syrian started the Mercedes. He would now take his hidden 'freight' to the border crossing at Checkpoint Charlie. And tomorrow the whole routine would be repeated. It was a crazy situation.

Back in the tram after a half-hour trek, I looked around discreetly. No one seemed to be watching me. But the plump woman with the huge shopping bag, could she be working for the Stasi? The bag could easily have been hiding a camera. Was I imagining things? The border officer at Heinrich Heine Strasse let me pass without a problem and stamped my day visa unhesitatingly. Back in West Berlin, I disappeared into the night.

A couple of hours later in a small apartment in Lichterfelde, I lay totally exhausted in Gudrun's arms. Fortunately, she asked no questions, as though she knew of the secret behind my irregular trips to East Berlin at short notice. I retreated into the seductive fragrance of her hair. But my thoughts were already wandering to the escape planned for tomorrow. If all would go well, the family would be reunited in the evening - in freedom. And I would be back with Gudrun, for another night. What time are you coming tomorrow? She didn't ask that question either.

ADVENTURER WITH A SENSE OF JUSTICE

The March sun was still somewhat pale, but the harbingers of spring were already appearing at the edges of the autobahn. A few blossoms peeked out here and there from the otherwise drab vegetation along the roadside. Full of joyful anticipation, I drove my Volkswagen, with its divided rear window, towards Berlin. The car was crammed full to the roof with books, clothing, bedding, and crockery. It was a long drive, but the 1949 VW Beetle gave me no trouble at all.

Three eventful semesters of law in Heidelberg lay behind me - much singing and plenty of drinking in the beer hall of our early nineteenth-century fraternity house, duelling with sharp foils, enjoying wonderful trips, and studying little. But now, in the spring of 1965, I wanted to leave this merry enclave and move on to experience something else, above all, studying seriously. Like so many others at that time, I was drawn to Berlin, and the government in Bonn subsidised two semesters of study in the divided city. I didn't want to let this chance slip by. To me, Berlin sounded like a call to adventure and freedom.

One problem I had not reckoned with delayed my arrival in West Berlin, however. Whereas West German autobahns were clearly signposted, I promptly got lost on one of the GDR transit routes. The road's cracked surface made for a rough ride; pine forests and fields alternated along the way. I drove and drove and soon no longer had any idea where I was. I had no street map with me. Why should I? I had never needed one in the West. There had not really been much traffic on the GDR autobahn for a while, but suddenly I realised that there were absolutely no cars coming in the opposite direction any more and that no other vehicle was in sight anywhere on my side either. Where in the world was I? Looking around anxiously, I eventually came across an East German police car on a parking area. Self-confident and fearless as I was, I assumed that the officers inside would surely help me.

I pulled up directly behind their car, got out, and bent down to speak to the two men, who had meanwhile rolled down their side window. 'Good afternoon, officers,' I began cheerfully. 'Please excuse me, but I'm afraid I'm totally lost. What is the best way for me to get from here to West Berlin?'

The officer in the passenger seat frowned in surprise and barked, 'You have no right to travel on this road, young man.' I looked at him, baffled, but before I could respond there followed a lengthy lecture about traffic laws and regulations. He then studied my papers thoroughly. Leaving the transit route without written permission was strictly forbidden. I did know that, but is it a criminal offence if a person unintentionally takes a wrong turn? When the policeman had finished his sermon, I thanked him politely for his information and asked with feigned innocence: 'Could you now perhaps tell me how to get back onto the right road?'

The question elicited additional highly complicated explanations that I could not comprehend, no matter how closely I listened. To avoid inviting any further antagonism from the two policemen, I refrained from asking them to repeat the directions. I gazed at them with apparent bewilderment, inquiring, 'Excuse me, but wouldn't it be the easiest just to turn around here? This autobahn only has a grassy centre median. That should do it.'

The two officers looked first at me and then for a long time at each other. Finally, the ranking officer, the driver, said, 'All right, turn around. But watch out for oncoming traffic when you cross the median strip!'

Oncoming traffic? I wanted to laugh out loud, but I pulled myself together and thanked them for their assistance in an exceptionally polite manner, as well as for their kind permission to turn around. Sitting in my car again, having crossed the median strip and now driving in the opposite direction, I could not suppress my laughter any longer. Welcome to the Prussian, comical, and yet humourless GDR!

The border check in Dreilinden seemed to me like a police vendetta. Had they telephoned ahead about my arrival? I had to drag my car's entire load, piece by piece, into a barrack about 15 metres (50 feet) away for detailed inspection, and then haul it all back again. The procedure took three and a half hours. I learned that patience and respect were needed – and very effective – when dealing with the GDR.

* * *

I rented a small room in a boarding house at 1 Argentinische Allee in the district of Zehlendorf, only a short drive from the Free University. During the subsequent weeks, I explored the 'front-line' city of Berlin. The place had a politically explosive quality. The Soviet Union and the United States saw their respective sector of Berlin as spearheading the struggle against each other's system. They both engaged in spying, blackmail, intrigue, intimidation, and deception. Blatant propaganda by the one and the other was part of life in Berlin, and the politically strained situation was palpable everywhere. On my walks through the city, I often took routes along the unsightly wall, which truncated or mutilated nearly two hundred streets. What a contrast to the tranquillity of Heidelberg, the paragon of Badenese cheerfulness.

I had registered to study political economics and law at the Free University (often abbreviated as FU) in Berlin. This university, a donation by the US, had been built in 1948 at the beginning East-West conflict as a counterpart to the communist Humboldt University in East Berlin and was characterised by a highly politicised student body. Aside from extensively exploring the city, I was looking for social contact. At Heidelberg University I belonged to the oldest student fraternity, the Corps Suevia. It had been founded in 1810 and, like many other such organisations, was essentially a child of the French Revolution and the German liberation movement. As a young man, I was drawn to being affiliated with a community that valued solidarity and conviviality.

On Hammersteinstrasse in Dahlem, a part of West Berlin in which the FU was located, I found the house of an affiliated fraternity called Lusatia Leipzig zu Berlin. Members of such student organisations could tap into the nationwide network of affiliated fraternities. I quickly made friends in Lusatia, among them Manfred Baum, a tall medical student with dark-blond hair and alert, blue-grey eyes. At that time I had no inkling of the extraordinary consequences that this encounter would have on my life.

After I had been in Berlin for about three or four months, I visited Manfred one day in his student flat on Köhlerstrasse in Lichterfelde-West in the neighbouring district of Steglitz. The place was not a typical Berlin block of rented flats but a smaller house in a suburb populated by many blue-collar workers and railroad men with their families. A married couple named Ahrens lived on the first floor and rented the basement rooms to students. Manfred was studying medicine. Something had seemed to be dispiriting him for some time, but I had not yet found out what it was and did not want to press him.

While Manfred boiled the water for a cup of coffee, I randomly picked up a magazine from the table. It was *Stern*, an illustrated news weekly published in Hamburg. I opened it somewhere in the middle and came across a series of photos that immediately gripped me. The pictures were part of an article about a spectacular escape operation. I could make out a truck and a giant folding ladder straddling a wall. The article was unmistakably about what GDR jargon referred to as the 'antifascist protective wall', which since August 1961 had constituted part of the system of border fortifications built by the GDR, a communist state that many people in the West simply called the 'Zone'. The intra-German border was 1,378 kilometres (856 miles) long. In 1965, however, the border and the Wall had not yet been made almost insurmountable by minefields and barbed wire, and the order to shoot anyone who tried to cross the barriers still lay in the distant future (the order did not formally become law until 1982). Escape by truck and retractable ladder was therefore still feasible in carefully chosen locations.

Buildings were recognisable in the pictures, but they were not in the centre of Berlin; the Wall was under especially close surveillance there. The photographs must have been taken on the outskirts, which were less strictly guarded.

From the accompanying text I learned that the escape had taken place on the grounds of a desolate cemetery. The article described the masterful way in which everything had been engineered, for it had involved a swivel ladder mounted on a truck. It was sensational. It was not for nothing that the escape had excited so much attention that news of it had found its way into *Stern*.

I was instantly fascinated by this bold operation and examined the pictures closely. We were living here smack in the middle of the Cold War. West Berlin universities in particular were highly politicised, mostly because of the Vietnam War and the division of the city. At that time everyone at the university was talking about these issues, no matter how uninterested they might be in other political issues. I too had been pondering for quite a while whether it wasn't a moral duty to help those who wanted to flee the GDR. I felt it was a great injustice that people on the other side of the Wall did not have the right of free movement.

Suddenly, I stopped. It couldn't be true. I examined the magazine closely. Yes, no doubt about it. One of the people assisting in the escape was definitely Manfred, although his name did not appear in the caption. It was the Manfred who was now sitting opposite me pouring freshly brewed coffee into chipped cups for the two of us. There was no doubt, it was Manfred's figure, sharply etched. The photo had been taken as he was helping a person climb down the ladder on the western side. That made sense because in such a tense situation a refugee was in danger of missing a rung and badly injuring himself.

'Manfred, that's you in the photo!' I exclaimed in amazement.

My new friend peered at me, then dismissed the comment with a wave of his hand.

'What, me? Nonsense.' He glanced at the photo. 'The man does look a bit like me, but that's the only connection between the two of us.'

'Manfred, please, take a proper look. You can't fool me. I'm not blind. That's you in the pictures. I'm not buying your yarn about doppelgängers!'

Thus it went back and forth for a while until Manfred gave up at last, exhausted. 'Volker, you're really nerve-racking. Why do you keep pounding away at it? Yes, I'm the guy in the photo. Satisfied?'

Satisfied? No way! I now bombarded him with ever more questions: 'Why were you there? What was your role?' Naturally, I had long since grasped what kind of operation he had engaged in. Manfred seemed both nervous and defiant.

'I help people escape,' my friend said outright.

'What? An escape helper? You'll have to spell that out for me.'

Manfred explained that he felt a strong sense of responsibility to help people from the GDR gain freedom if they no longer wanted to live there. And after some hesitation he added, 'I started by building tunnels but unfortunately our last tunnel was discovered.'

I was fired up. And deeply impressed. It all sounded like a big adventure, one in which people were being helped!

'Come on, you can't leave it at that. Tell me what it's all about,' I prompted. 'Don't say you were one of those involved in that famous Tunnel 57 discovered a few months ago?' I had read about it in the papers. The tunnel was named after the number of people who had crawled through it to freedom on 3 October 1964.

He nodded modestly. 'Yes, exactly that. I was one of the diggers. There were thirty-five of us in all. Our leader was Wolfgang Fuchs, "The Tunnel Fox", as he was called in the papers.'

'Yes, I've heard the name before,' I confirmed excitedly.

'The Fox is known in the relevant circles. He recruited me, too. And he thought up the deal with the ladder.'

Everything I was hearing impressed me a lot.

'How long was your tunnel?' I probed a bit deeper.

'Just over 145 metres (475 feet) long and 12 metres (39 feet) deep.'

'Manfred, please, don't force me to worm every answer out of you. Or are you vowed to secrecy?'

'Well,' said Manfred slowly, 'a lot has already been made public, so the whole thing is not really secret any more. What I can say for sure: We started our digging on the western side in the basement of an abandoned bakery on Bernauer Strasse, then went under the Wall and ended in the courtyard of a derelict outhouse at 55 Strelitzer Strasse. That was poor planning, unfortunately, because we actually wanted to come out in the basement.'

'How long did you burrow underground? You couldn't use any machines – and 145 metres is an incredibly long stretch!' I gazed at Manfred. He was not only tall, he also had a strong build. How could a person work in a narrow tunnel without suffering from claustrophobia? In his shoes I would have.

'Hmm. It took about seven months, and we were all volunteers. We started with shovels and buckets in April 1964, the first 57 escapees managed to pass through it to the West in early October. The next operation was already planned for about midnight the next day, but some of the refugees were actually working for the Ministry of State Security. That was the end of it.'

'And how did the Stasi come into the picture?'

I suppose the question had finally pushed things too far. Without answering it, Manfred changed the topic. But I did not let up and managed to wheedle out of him what he had initially not wanted to reveal. On Strelitzer Strasse there had been an exchange of shots involving a different tunnel digger, Reinhard Furrer, a native North Tyrolean who later became West Germany's first astronaut. Furrer, too, was a student at the Free University and had participated in several escape operations, including Tunnel 57. During the night of the 4/5 October, he had waited at the tunnel's eastern opening to assist the refugees as they entered it. At the last minute some Stasi operatives, presumably tipped off by a resident or a remorseful would-be-escapee, claimed to be going to fetch a friend, but returned instead with border guards. When the escape helpers noticed the danger and ran back to the tunnel, someone in the group lost his nerve and fired in the direction of the soldiers, hitting one of them: Egon Schultz. He fell at once, mortally wounded. Why had Egon Schultz been shot at? Who had fired the fatal bullet? In all likelihood it could only have been one of the escape helpers. We didn't know then that an NVA border guard had killed him accidentally in the nocturnal crossfire. That came out only decades later from autopsy documents kept secret by the Stasi. For a quarter of a century, the allegedly fatal shot weighed heavily on the group of escape helpers, especially on the one who fired his pistol. With East German state pomp, Erich Honecker accompanied the victim's mother to her son's funeral, fulminating against the capitalist murderers, knowing full well that one of his own people had accidentally shot Egon Schultz. Criminal proceedings in West-Berlin were abandoned because the GDR refused to make the autopsy available.

I began to delve further into the topic of escape aid. Wolfgang Fuchs had not been the first to come up with the idea of tunnelling. In 1962 Hasso Herschel, who came from Dresden and had fled to the West with a false passport in 1961, wanted to help his sister and her whole family flee. He and about thirty others dug a tunnel 394 feet (120 metres) from Bernauer Strasse in the West to Schönholzer Strasse in the East. He had gone about this project prudently and intelligently. He was a born organiser (a description befitting Wolfgang Fuchs as well, but Fuchs tended to be a daredevil, not as restrained and disciplined as Herschel). In September 1962 twenty-nine people, including Herschel's sister, escaped to the West through the tunnel. There were additional escapes of this kind on a smaller scale, but Tunnel 29 and Tunnel 57 were the biggest such projects.

To Manfred's dismay, my enthusiasm mounted. 'And who financed all this digging? Or did everyone do it for nothing? How was it with you folks?'

Manfred did not respond much to these questions, either. 'It is known that Herschel and two Italian students helping him cooperated with the American broadcasting station NBC, selling it the film rights.'

'Did that also happen with Tunnel 57?'

Again, he beat around the bush. 'Sort of. I don't know exactly.'

'Were there financial problems?' I could be tenacious when I wanted to. And in this case, I wanted to.

'Yes, now and then these issues would crop up. Money came from individuals. I don't know more than that, honestly.'

'Uh-huh,' was all I replied.

I found out only much later that that these individuals were close to, or even members of, the Christian Democratic Union (CDU).

They presumably included Ernst Lemmer, who was West Germany's Minister for Displaced Persons, Refugees, and War Victims, and Fritz Amrehn, a member of the Berlin House of Representatives. Both Lemmer and Amrehen wanted to provide political support for efforts to help people escape from East Germany. The largest donation was DM 30,000 (about $7,500 in the 1960s), a sizeable sum at that time. Behind the scenes was the so-called secret fund of West Germany's Federal Ministry for All-German Affairs[1] – money that it approved and did not have to publicly disclose. The government used the fund for operations to help people escape. Not without a quid pro quo, however. The donors had particular wishes as far as the selection of refugees was concerned. Nevertheless, as several tunnel builders later independently swore to me, every penny of the money received went into the project. The escape helpers themselves, Manfred assured me, were not paid. In a sense, it was a code of honour. You did not do it for money. I had my doubts about that, though. I couldn't really imagine that all the financial resources had been spent exclusively on tunnel building material. But these reservations were quickly forgotten. I liked the idea of the code of honour all too much. As a member of my fraternity, I had accepted its 'comment', the rules we had to abide by, and there were consequences for violating them. Voluntary commitment meant a great deal to me even then, as it still does today. The senior students were to look after and, if necessary, protect the first-year student members, the 'foxes.' That aspect appealed to me a lot.

There was still something else going through my mind, and I brought it up. Poor Manfred, I really had him cornered. 'If the

---

1 This office addressed East and West German issues of interest to the West German government.

tunnelling efforts have been only partially successful, is their time over now?' After all, the digging took months with so many people lying in the mud and shovelling. How and where were the immense amounts of earth stored in the meantime? That needed space. Moreover, there was the fear that the GDR border guards would be closely watching certain activities after every operation that had its cover blown. How often had I seen newspaper photos in which the guards scrutinised everything with huge binoculars? Surely, they had more than just state-of-the art optical equipment. I could well imagine that their ears, too, were well trained to localise any anomalous acoustical signal.

Manfred shrugged his shoulders while he took a sip of his now cold coffee. 'Honestly, I really can't tell you in so much detail.'

'I understand,' I said. 'But I want you to know that I find what you're doing really fantastic.'

Manfred smiled. But it was true. I found it absolutely marvellous that he was helping other people and running a high risk in doing so. To me, it was the epitome of civil courage. All parties of the federal government at the time agreed that the building of the Wall had been an inhumane act. Unquestionably. It seemed to me that no one actually wanted it, except the Soviet Union and the other COMECON states (the socialist counterpart to the states of the European Economic Community), including the GDR, a small number of socialist African and Arab states, and a few supporters of Communist groups in the policy-making community or at university.

The basic political attitude in the West, however, was pretty clear: The GDR was a dictatorial system, and the people living under it were suffering. Of course, there were exceptions, especially among those maintaining that system.

West Berlin in the 1960s was a largely isolated, truncated city pervaded by a subversive atmosphere and the constant feeling of being under threat. In Moscow Nikita Khrushchev held power until 1964, and if something did not suit him, he had fighter planes take off in the vicinity of Berlin and repeatedly break the sound barrier in a bid to intimidate the population. Noise terrorism.

The mood was tense. The Cuban crisis of 1962 still cast its shadow. The average citizen, too, felt this stress at the border checkpoints in Berlin. Cars and people were regularly searched, which could take hours. I had experienced it myself. It would be a long time before détente gradually set in. The *Ostverträge* of the 1970s – the political, economic, and social agreements between West Germany and some countries of the Eastern bloc to achieve change through rapprochement and normal neighbourly relations – still lay in the distant future.

Manfred's stories occupied my mind a great deal. His actions demanded a lot of courage, and it was in principle a sort of resistance he was waging against the GDR. A few parallels between the two of us occurred to me. Like him, I came from a conservative parental home. We were both members of a fencing fraternity with basically conservative structures. But I had never simply adopted political positions without first looking into them. The question of where I actually stood was crucial to me. And I always acted according to my own convictions, sometimes disappointing my father, the head of engineering at Glanzstoff AG in Wuppertal-Elberfeld. He wished for his son to become an engineer like himself. But after graduation from secondary school, six months of practical training in Scotland and England and two semesters of mechanical engineering in Karlsruhe,

I decided to study law. I feel especially drawn to helping others as a lawyer, and this aspiration was to mark my initial years in that profession. I specialised in landlord and tenant law, always representing tenants, never landlords. This involvement on behalf of others, especially for the weaker, has been a desire of mine since childhood. If one of my siblings or friends suffered an injustice, I instantly felt compelled to intervene and see justice done, even if it was only about someone taking more than their fair share of food at the table. That was why I found the fraternity's clause about protecting the junior students pivotal. Much later, as the Corps' president, I suggested fraternities do charitable community work as well – sadly, a proposal not met with approval.

When I lived in West Berlin, Willy Brandt was chairman of the Social Democratic Party of Germany (SPD) and simultaneously Governing Mayor of West Berlin. I was an enthusiastic supporter of Brandt, who shaped my political convictions more than anyone else. In hindsight, I can only agree with his policy of mutual recognition, increased trade across political borders and the gradual elimination of travel restrictions by the east European communist countries, in particular the GDR. Continuing to help people escape from East Germany, or buying the freedom of GDR citizens on a grand scale, would only have led to draining that country economically more and more. And for those left behind it would have meant 'bad luck that you couldn't get out.' In my eyes, these *Ostverträge* were supremely humanitarian treaties.

I was prepared to help with the escapes. But would I countenance use of a weapon if the worst came to the worst? I thought of the duels in the fraternity. To me, academic fencing by students using sharp weapons – a traditional, strictly regulated fight with foils known as *Mensur*, which still survives at some German universities, was primarily a test of valour. This student variety of fencing is more sport than combat, though I must admit that some of its characteristics, such as the rule that one is never allowed to dodge or flinch, seem somewhat peculiar to the uninitiated. In the end it is a test of courage and proof of solidarity. I simply enjoyed fencing. Many others did it because it was the non-negotiable price of full membership in the fraternity. All the better if you had fun doing it. And I did. But carrying a weapon, a firearm, that was quite another thing. I couldn't say for certain how much self-control a person had when in danger. I knew only that I wanted nothing to do with weapons.

The political situation of West Berlin concerned me a lot, and I felt as though I had my finger on the pulse of history. And now the chance to act was presenting itself to me. Was there a financial motive? No. My parents were sending me monthly cheques, which sufficed to make ends meet for a student. A humanitarian motive? Yes, there certainly was that, along with a hankering for adventure. I was young, the world was open to me – and I wanted to change something. Then I heard myself say to Manfred two sentences that were to change my life: 'I'd like to join you. You can count on me.' I was a bit surprised myself when the words came out.

At first Manfred said nothing, then he gave me a penetrating look.

'You do understand the possible consequences, don't you?'

'Of course,' I responded firmly.

'Are you aware that they won't take you on board just like that? You'll be put to the test.'

'Anything else would be irresponsible,' I countered.

'But some think they'll immediately get to help build a tunnel or something spectacular of that sort.'

I shrugged. 'I'll wait and see.'

'OK, I just wanted to warn you.'

'And how will I be tested?' I found that more exciting.

'You'll call on someone in East Berlin to whom you'll then give a coded message. Just running errands, being a courier.'

'Do I know what kind of message it is?'

'Usually not. But sometimes it's only about asking whether the person is still interested.'

'In what way interested?'

'Well, if he still wants to come over to the West. These operations have a lengthy lead time. In the meantime, the person may have changed his mind.'

Many of the inexperienced couriers, I learned later, were caught on their first assignment. Professional escape helpers, who did this business for purely commercial reasons, took advantage of students who had shown a certain enthusiasm and willingness but who had subsequently not been well instructed, if at all. If they got into difficulties, they had to handle it alone. In Berlin, and in the GDR generally, there were few public telephones from which to call the West. And they were bound to be monitored. Whoever operated as an escape helper in the GDR had to know that he was completely on his own.

'Are you trying to scare me off?' I asked.

'No,' said Manfred. 'But you should know what you're getting yourself into.'

CODED MESSAGES

For a long time I heard nothing. It was unsettling. Had I not clearly shown my willingness? But there was only dead silence. I went to university, occasionally relaxed in student pubs, played chess, often went to the theatre and the cinema, attended concerts, and debated with my fellow students the escalating crisis at the universities and the menacing political situation of West Berlin. I was already in my second semester there and had long since come to believe that the whole affair would come to nothing, when matters began to move.

'Volker, Wolfgang Fuchs wants to meet you,' Manfred told me one evening while we were sitting once again in the Hammersteinstrasse beer hall.

'Where?'

'Tonight, at Fatso's.'

'For heaven's sake, who is Fatso?'

'That's what we call the pub on my street. Its real name is "Zum Dicken."'

The name was justified, it was run by a portly barkeeper. His partner was a bit less corpulent, though still chubby. She was very likeable; he, rather grumpy. Their establishment was a cross between a working class and a students' pub, with a pinball machine and reasonably priced beverages. Hungry patrons ordered hard-boiled pickled eggs with potato salad. Everybody smoked; thick haze and dim lamps submerged the bar in a wan light. The main drink was beer, accompanied by small glasses filled with corn schnapps or Persiko, a reddish liquor which brightened up the mood. Daughters of the upper crust did not come into this pub, which tended to be frequented by ladies with chequered backgrounds who attracted men of all ages.

Seated at a table in this boisterous and jovial milieu was Fuchs with a glass of beer in front of him. I immediately noticed his engaging manner. He was about 1.85 metres tall (6 foot 2) and his medium-sized beer belly shook when he laughed. That happened quite often because he had a great sense of humour. His dark hair was closely cropped, and there was no hint of vanity about him. Fuchs was clearly a mover and shaker, someone who took action and didn't indulge in endless philosophising.

Before we met in the autumn of 1965, probably in October or November, I had of course done some research. Wolfgang Fuchs was born in 1939 and was a trained optician from Jena. He and his wife Selina were visiting West Berlin when the Wall went up. Selina had returned to their children in the GDR, however, not wanting to leave them behind alone. Fuchs thought about how he could help his family escape. He soon came up with an unusual idea. In March 1962 he managed to bring Selina and the two children over the Wall by using ladders while helpers threw Molotov cocktails to distract the Berlin NVA border guards. Afterwards, he focused increasingly on building tunnels, besides some individual operations, and brought additional family members and friends to the West. I found his motives credible: like most people organising escapes, he had come into conflict with the authorities in the GDR, his homeland. All the escape helpers hated the communist system. It was the same with Hasso Herschel. This hatred had not paralysed them but rather spurred them on. They refused to accept what the state agencies of the GDR were doing to its young citizens hungry for freedom. They did not want to debate; they wanted to act.

As former GDR citizens, they had the advantage of being thoroughly familiar with the localities, the milieu, and the communist system and thus knew incomparably more than a West German student like I did. The key point was that not only was Fuchs motivated himself, but he was able to motivate others, like an officer leading his troops into battle. After the sensational success with Tunnel 57, he had an immense reputation. To many in the scene, he was a hero. When people asked who could be trusted on the market of escape helpers, his name would have been high on the list.

I liked Fuchs straight away. After a bit of small talk, we quickly delved into a proper conversation, and together we considered how future escapes could be organised and, after the discovery of Tunnel 57, whether digging tunnels was still promising.

'How do you actually make contact with the people who want to escape?' I enquired, taking a sip of my beer. We addressed each other with the informal *du* from the start; whoever sat together at Fatso's dispensed with formalities.

'Through Rainer Hildebrandt. He founded the Wall museum at Checkpoint Charlie in 1963. Does that ring a bell?'

'Sure,' I replied. I knew that Hildebrandt had initially set up an exhibition about the building of the Wall, later expanding it by documenting successful or abortive attempts to escape. 'But how can you be certain that he won't betray you or come into contact with the wrong people?'

'How can I be sure? I can't. But I don't question him. Rainer shares my hatred of the Zone.'

'Is that really enough?'

'I have to distrust many people, but if I distrust everyone, I can just give up.'

'Understood.'

We talked about every conceivable aspect of helping people to escape, though everyday topics also came up as our drinking continued. Fuchs was mostly concerned with sizing me up. He studied me closely. Finally, he said, 'I can already tell you: I like you. I think you could fit well into our group.'

By now my face flushed and my head foggy, I ventured cautiously: 'Does that sort of mean I've passed the test?'

'Right, test passed. In the coming days you can begin as a messenger.'

Three days later Fuchs gave me an oral coded message – 'Call your grandmother' – and specified a meeting point on a platform at the Strausberger Platz underground station in Friedrichshain, where the coded message was to be passed on to a man. 'You'll recognise him by the blue volume of Karl Marx's works he'll be carrying under his arm. And don't get the idea of writing the message on a piece of paper. It's so simple, you can certainly memorise it!'

'And what does the message mean?'

'You don't need to know that, but it will make sense to the recipient. He knows what to do with it.'

Naturally, I would have liked to learn more, but I pulled myself together. I trusted Fuchs, and if I wanted to join the operation,

I had to get used to casting aside doubts. I understood that part of a messenger's job was to know as little as possible so as to avoid endangering myself or others. You could come through adventures only if you were ready to put your own interests last.

'Everyone in East Berlin is bound to see that I come from the West. Wouldn't it be better if I wore GDR clothes?'

Fuchs laughed, his belly shaking vigorously. 'Even if you do put on garb like that, everyone will still see you're not from the GDR. Just be yourself. You'll stick out least if you come across naturally. Don't do anything artificial! It's as simple as that.'

'I'm so glad I can wear my own clothes. Are there any other rules for how to behave?'

'No, you'll just have to find your own style. Simply be alert, observe keenly, but don't let it show.'

I was still not quite satisfied. 'And why Strausberger Platz rather than Friedrichstrasse, which is teeming with people? It's easy to mingle with the crowd there and innocuously wait for the train.'

Fuchs gave a deep, audible sigh. I seemed to be thinking far too much.

'Friedrichstrasse is a border checkpoint. It is crammed full of Stasi people; you'll notice that quickly enough. The departure hall there isn't called the "Palace of Tears" for nothing. Forget Friedrichstrasse; forget all other checkpoints, too. That's unprofessional.'

I accepted that. I had no doubt at that moment that Fuchs was a consummate professional. Two days later I entered East Berlin through the Friedrichstrasse checkpoint on a day visa. From there I intended to walk to Karl Marx Allee, where the Strausberger Platz underground station was located. I could have taken the underground, but I wanted to familiarise myself better with East

Berlin, a process best done on foot. I was tense. I was aware that I had to behave as inconspicuously as possible, but my body did not completely cooperate. I somehow felt I'd swallowed a rod, and I was sure that anyone even ten metres away could tell that I was up to something. I observed the tiniest details, things a normal pedestrian would not perceive at all. Over-attentive, always reckoning with a threat. I saw ghosts. My brain conjured up dangerous situations that objectively did not exist. I could not altogether trust my own senses.

To keep my cool, I tried to concentrate on something quite different. Unfortunately, I couldn't come up with anything better to think about than a class trip years earlier. I was seventeen then, and on one of the days we travelled to East Berlin because our teacher very much wanted to show us the Pergamon museum. After we had admired the Babylonian and Greek artwork, I'd had enough of being part of a large group supervised by our unpopular teacher of Ancient Greek. I slipped away and walked alone through the streets, which were largely devoid of cars and lined with many buildings destroyed or damaged in the war. I was amazed how little colour I saw. I remember an ocean of grey tones and a sense of bleakness. Only the imposing Prussian buildings in the city centre attracted my attention. When it was time to head back to the youth hostel in the West, I walked to the Friedrichstrasse underground station where we had entered. The Wall did not exist yet, nor did regular border checks.

'Where is your visa?' the border guard demanded.

'I don't have one,' I told him truthfully.

'But you did enter East Berlin, didn't you?' The officer's voice took on a menacing undertone.

'Yes, I did, with my class. But unfortunately I lost track of them along the way.' I tried to look innocent.

'Come with me.' His voice now sounded even more ominous.

I was led into a bunker-like room and interrogated for at least four hours. They posed the same questions again and again ('Why did you leave your class?' 'What were you doing the past two hours?' 'Where did you go?'). Eventually, I was allowed to leave.

That actually should have been a warning to me. But it was far too late. Apparently, I loved tests of courage, just as I loved the duels with sharp foils in the fraternity. Of course, you could sustain facial injuries, but they healed. My father had a few fencing scars on the left side of his face from his student days. Luckily, I escaped without any. But now I was about to pass quite a different test of courage. I did not shrink from what others did not dare to do. That lent me inner satisfaction as a young man – in defiance of all the ghosts and fears.

At that moment I saw the Strausberger Platz underground station. On the platform I quickly discovered the man with a volume of Karl Marx in his hand. I should perhaps read it someday, too, I thought as I approached him. It was not by chance that I had left the group during my school excursion to East Berlin in order to get my own impression of communist East Berlin alone and undisturbed by others.

'Call your grandmother,' I muttered as I passed by. Just loud enough that he could hear me.

The man nodded and then went off in the opposite direction. That's it, I thought. Feeling relieved, I took the underground back to the border crossing at Friedrichstrasse. I had done it. All the pursuers I had imagined dissolved into thin air. Test of courage passed. I sat relaxed at the window; house façades raced by outside. What might the news mean that I had passed on?

'I don't think it's clever to enter specified buildings or apartments to deliver messages,' I said one day to Wolfgang after delivering yet another message as a courier. 'It makes the destination clearly identifiable and thus not totally safe for anyone involved.'

'True. But meeting in a bar at Alexanderplatz or in Café Moscow isn't any better,' Fuchs answered. 'You always have to assume that the people at the next table have big ears.'

'But we can invite the person for coffee and pass on the message while taking a walk with him afterwards. That would be much wiser.'

Fuchs thought about it. 'Maybe I should give you more demanding missions,' he said finally. 'What do you think?'

'I'm fine with that.'

I did not deliver many coded messages. Fuchs had rapidly come to feel that he could use me better for other things. Things that required more courage: assisting with escapes themselves. Perhaps, though, I had only annoyed him with my suggestions for passing on messages. It was all the same to me. I had accomplished what had been on my mind ever since the conversation with Manfred: I did not want to remain at the lowest operational level.

* * *

It was the heyday of Rudi Dutschke at that time. He was one of the most important people in the student protest movement in West Berlin after the Wall was built. He gave stirring speeches with his large megaphone. He had a very aggressive voice, and everything he said sounded to me like slogans. He especially condemned the Vietnam War, with its napalm attacks on military targets and the civilian population, a conflict that had dragged on for years. I definitely shared his sentiments. But I did not like the general condemnation of the Americans. How foolish, I thought. America is the only power that can really keep protecting West Berlin, diplomatically and militarily. Thousands of US soldiers were stationed in the city, and 1,500 more troops arrived as reinforcements after the Wall went up. They showed their presence. They were clearly visible to every West Berlin citizen and on television to every GDR citizen. When US President John F. Kennedy was in Berlin in June 1963, his criticism of the Wall was limited – better the Wall than another war, he said.

I found it grotesque how Dutschke demonised the Americans without realising that he could not be exercising his political right of free speech in the first place without their presence in West Berlin. I recall a day when I was on my way to East Berlin. As I rode past the Free University, Dutschke was ranting into his megaphone again at the main auditorium's forecourt. It occurred to me, not without a certain degree of satisfaction: you talk, I act.

We escape helpers wanted to achieve something, but what? After the Wall was built, there were no more personal encounters between East and West Berliners. Only foreigners (via Checkpoint Charlie) or Germans holding a personal identity card issued in the West were allowed to enter through the few border crossings. Members of separated families could not see each other at all for nearly two and a half years. Not until 17 December 1963 was a temporary travel-permit agreement signed. From 19 December 1963 through 5 January 1964 – including Christmas and New Year's Eve – approximately 700,000 people had applied for such passes. By 1966 three additional agreements of this kind were to follow. These agreements were brokered by Horst Korber, a negotiator of the Senate of West Berlin, which the GDR regarded as a separate political unit, and East Germany's Undersecretary of State, Erich Wendt. There were no official contacts between the Federal Republic of Germany and the GDR, so negotiators with powers of attorney were used. In West Berlin the checkpoints were initially staffed not by police officers but by postal employees. Everything advanced at a glacial pace.

We were not politicians. We did not want to bring about occasional encounters for everyone but rather freedom for real persons who longed for it. Of course, given the East German population of 16 million people, what we were doing was only a drop in the ocean.

What distinguished me from Dutschke? Actually, I could have identified with him. I had graduated from secondary school in 1962, so, like him, I had gone to school in the 1950s. Ten years later I would surely have created a labour union for school students. At that time, however, I was not yet able to voice intelligent criticism of my teachers, a few of whom could not sufficiently conceal their Nazi past. But because I could not yet politically process the reality of the Nazis, I communicated my rejection by playing the rebel. I set fire to the Advent wreath at school, I tore a wash basin from the wall and flooded the classroom. The acts were manifestations of enormous personal frustration, and I went to incredible lengths to vent it. The school principal, who was my French teacher, asked me woefully, 'How can such an intelligent young man behave so grotesquely?' He was right, I knew it myself but said nothing.

A few weeks before my final exams at school, my father had to appear before the school authorities in Düsseldorf to plead with them to retract my expulsion for serious misconduct and instead to reprimand me formally so that I could take my exams. It could not have been easy for him. Maybe he only did it for my mother's sake.

My mother had been forced to drop out of school to work as a secretary at the age of seventeen after the early death of her father, who had been seriously wounded in the First World War. She had married my father in 1940, when she was twenty-two. He was twelve years her senior. My father was the son of a farmer who only through great personal sacrifice had enabled his son to complete a master's degree in engineering. After graduating, my father was an employee at Spinnfaser Stock Corporation (AG) in Kassel, where I was born. He then joined Dynamit Nobel AG. Shortly after the Second World War he worked on his father's farm, then started at Glanzstoff AG in Wuppertal-Elberfeld where he eventually became the director of engineering. Our family lived in relative prosperity, and my parents urged us to take our education seriously. I was their second child, with an older sister, a younger brother and sister, and two cousins about my age who had lost their parents in tragic war-related circumstances not long after the war.

I now nevertheless took my law studies less seriously than my work for Fuchs. I mentally waved to Dutschke as I continued on my way to the border. I wondered whether I could recruit him as an escape helper – and immediately answered myself. No, he wanted big politics, I wanted direct help for individual people.

***

'Do you think I'm under surveillance in East Berlin?' I asked Manfred whilst sitting with him and other escape helpers in a pub one evening. Everyone at the table had worked on Tunnel 57, but none had actively taken part in such operations since then. I was about to join in earnest, I wanted to become more deeply involved.

'Of course they can watch you, but the problem is you don't know it. No one knows anything really definite. In any case, we always felt relatively safe as far as the western powers and the West Berlin Senate were concerned. I can't say for sure, but I'm convinced that the Senate and the western Allies were well aware of what was going on but didn't officially say so.'

'Actually, rather the opposite is the case,' interjected Joachim Schreiber, one of the others at the table. 'After the early discovery of the tunnel, the Senate informed us through emissaries that such operations should stop at least temporarily because they would jeopardise the conclusion of the next round of negotiations for travel permits. We were furious.' Schreiber had close contact with Wolfgang Fuchs. He, too, was a law student and was twenty-three years old when the tunnel was built. He was small and constantly on the move, an activist in the truest sense of the word. He felt – as did all the others – that the Wall was a huge injustice, and he wanted to bring over friends from the East who were not allowed to study in the West, which was still possible before the Wall was built. After attending lectures and seminars at the Free University, he had regularly dug for hours. He made sure that the support beams for the tunnel made it into the former bakery's basement unnoticed and ensured that they were properly installed. A colossal feat. When talking with him, I had the impression that he, too, had not done it for money.

'And because the Berlin Senate requested it,' I asked, 'you all gave up on the extremely hard work of building tunnels, with a few minor exceptions?'

'That's right. Some of us are taking a break, including me. Others are looking for alternatives.'

'I see that the standpoint of the Berlin Senate and the western Allies is understandable, but what about the GDR and the Soviet Union? How do they see it?'

'We're criminals to them,' said Manfred. Everyone laughed.

'That's clear to me, but what about the question of surveillance?'

Ulrich Bahnsen, another escape helper, explained: 'Everything that comes across as suspicious to them they register and immediately use for their propaganda purposes, of course. Look what happened after the NVA man was shot dead on Strelitzer Strasse. They claimed that it could only have been done by the evil westerners. No other possibility was even considered. But if things remain quiet, you can assume that the NVA or Stasi people don't know anything.'

Bahnsen also belonged to the inner circle and, like Schreiber, was studying law at the Free University. I had not met Bahnsen personally yet. He had been detained in the GDR, first in investigative custody in Berlin-Hohenschönhausen and then in prison for a comparatively brief period in Bautzen after conviction for 'assaults on the state frontier of the GDR'. In total, he had received a sentence of five or six years but had served only about one year of it. Now, in January 1966, he had just been released. Wolfgang, Manfred and others handled the release very secretively, and I felt excluded because I had actually come to see myself as a full member. But probably they simply wanted to protect their friend after that experience. Before we all gathered at Fatso's that evening, Fuchs and Manfred had been on vacation with Bahnsen on Mallorca. But when the three returned and all the mystery-mongering was over, Ulrich became one of my friends, too. An upstanding, clear-thinking, sensitive man with a good sense of humour, thick dark hair, and a thin, almost aristocratic face. From the outset I regarded him highly.

'Or they're waiting for the right moment to pounce,' Manfred weighed in. 'Those are the only two possibilities.'

'We have no reliable way of knowing what the western secret services and the western Allies think,' added Jürgen Kreuz. 'As far as I'm aware, though, the Americans, French, or British have never yet officially intervened against escape helpers.'

That was almost exactly what I had been thinking. Much seemed to be clear, but in the end nothing was clear after all. Over the course of the evening, I had the chance to talk briefly with Ulrich alone at the table.

'You were a tunnel builder and courier?' I asked.

He nodded, but added nothing, wanting first to find out whom he was really dealing with.

'Wasn't it quite tough?' He shrugged.

'But you were arrested when you were active in East Berlin as a courier?'

At last he spoke. Perhaps he had meanwhile made up his mind about me and instinctively trusted me. And maybe Fuchs had told him I could be trusted. 'Yeah; fortunately, no one could prove that I was building tunnels, otherwise I would definitely have received a longer sentence.'

'But you still got out pretty quickly. How come?' I did not seek details about why he had been convicted. Probably to protect myself. Had I known about too many unpleasant consequences, I might not have been able to carry out my own courier assignments so easily anymore.

'Wolfgang Vogel saw to it,' Ulrich explained tersely, wiping beer foam from his mouth.

'Who is that?' I wanted to know.

'A GDR lawyer. In 1962 he not only organised the first exchange of agents between the United States and the Soviet Union but was also a negotiator in buying or exchanging East and

West German citizens out of prison. By the way, his West Berlin counterpart is the lawyer Jürgen Stange.'

'Is that what happened in your case?' I pressed.

'Well...' Ulrich hesitated a bit before deciding to come out with the truth. 'As far as I know, money wasn't demanded as a quid pro quo for me. They sought instead the release of an East German citizen serving time in a West German prison.' This was really riveting. I was thirsty and ordered another beer for each of us right away.

'Was it like in a genuine spy thriller? In a covert kind of operation on a bridge?'

Ulrich laughed. 'I think you've been watching too many films. With me it was quite mundane. But you're right in a way. Vogel initiated the first exchange of agents at that time, on the Glienicke Bridge in Potsdam. It was in February 1962 as far as I remember.'

'And who was sent from the one side to the other?'

'First of all, cheers!' We toasted our new friendship, and Ulrich told me that the Americans had captured a KGB spy, Colonel Rudolf Ivanovich Abel, and the Russians had shot down a US pilot over the Urals. Francis Gary Powers had been flying a high-altitude reconnaissance mission. Abel was one of the most successful Soviet spies. He had betrayed American nuclear secrets and several other things. Such a man couldn't be left in the lurch, otherwise no one would want to risk their life anymore. Vogel made a name for himself in the relevant circles through this exchange. How could I have guessed that I was actually to meet him myself?

'A person like this Vogel must have strong nerves or he couldn't negotiate such deals,' I observed after Ulrich had finished his account. Just hearing this story of the man made him fascinating to me.

'Strong nerves, sure, but good connections are needed, too. Loyalty to the state is essential, of course. Without those attributes you can forget about having such a job as a lawyer in the GDR. If Vogel didn't exist, you'd have had to invent him.'

It was true. The lawyer seemed to be a figure with the requisite combination of both commendable and somewhat unsavoury qualities.

'If he helped you, then he apparently brokers deals not only with the Americans and Russians but with our own government, too, right?'

'Yes, but these exchange deals are not yet publicly known, and that's why I don't want to say anything more about them, as much as I'd like to.'

'OK, I understand. But tell me what it was like under arrest. It couldn't have been the most pleasant time for you. What happens in an East German jail? How does it differ from our system, if you're able to compare them at all?'

Ulrich gave a detailed account of the food, eternally the same stews, the sleeping times, the prison apparel, the weekly showers, the constant interrogations. When I later landed in jail myself and was able to confirm everything Ulrich had described, the shock was strangely limited. It was as though this conversation had prepared me.

A few days later I discussed with Wolfgang once again why tunnels had no future any more. It was an important topic to me because I was keen on doing something more challenging and on ending my role as a courier as soon as possible. A rumour was circulating that the GDR was now using or had already developed seismographic equipment that could detect subterranean activity. If that were true, it was much too dangerous to continue the time-consuming and expensive effort to build tunnels. But doing nothing was out of the question.

We were standing, as we often did, on one of the wooden lookout platforms in Kreuzberg, wrapped in heavy coats and scarves and with caps on our heads. We followed all the movements on the other side, making direct eye contact with the East Berlin border guards. Now and then they stared at us through oversized binoculars, an eerie scenario almost inviting us to take cover.

Wolfgang still could not come up with an idea as brilliant as the tunnelling operations had been.

'It might make sense to try escaping through neighbouring socialist countries,' I thought out loud while gazing at the television tower on Alexanderplatz.

Wolfgang had an instant rebuttal ready: 'It would be enormously complicated and far too unsafe for us to operate in Romania, Hungary, or Bulgaria. And don't forget, none of us speak the languages of those countries at even a beginner's level.'

'So what do you propose then?' I was gradually getting impatient. I wanted to do something at last.

'The old methods: forged passports and converted cars. They've always worked well.'

'Granted,' I countered, 'but the numbers are rather limited. And it should be something that works quickly and locally. Every car that crosses the border several times is much too conspicuous.'

'Do you have a better suggestion?' Wolfgang took a drag on his cigarette, which prompted me to light one, too. The first drag was always the best.

Yes, I had an idea. At least I thought so at that moment, for I had just seen American soldiers cross the border in a jeep. 'Listen, why don't we try doing it once with our Allied friends? They're never checked when they drive into the Russian sector.

Some of those jeeps have tarpaulin covers. They could easily take a few people along under there.' Sealing off the Soviet zone in Germany, including East Berlin, had not been initiated by the western Allies; it had been a unilateral measure taken by the GDR with explicit approval from the Soviet Union. However, the access routes remained open to all Allied forces. The British and Americans in particular used them and repeatedly made a point of driving into the Russian sector. My idea was simply splendid. In my opinion at any rate.

I looked at Wolfgang expectantly through a haze of cigarette smoke. His nose was red from the cold, and he looked unenthusiastic. I had expected a little more euphoria.

'What's the problem?' I asked. I couldn't understand his reserve.

'Well,' he paused, 'explaining the whole affair to the Allies would take good language skills – English or French. I personally had only Russian in school. I wouldn't be able to contribute much.'

'OK,' I said. 'If you want, I can take it on for you.' My father had regularly sent my siblings and me abroad during school and semester vacations in order to learn languages. I had returned only about a year earlier from a lengthy stay in Paris. I spoke pretty passable English and French.

Wolfgang still hesitated, but then made up his mind. 'OK. It's worth a try.'

Satisfied, I smiled. 'Then I'll go and march into the Allied barracks.' The military operation was thus decided. We smoked another cigarette in silence under the watchful eyes peering through binoculars.

BARRACKS AND CARPET DEALERS

Damn. There just had to be an opportune moment. Detective stories always had one in such situations. But as yet none had presented itself. Maybe because I was not the hero in a crime novel but instead was caught in the midst of Cold War reality. The guard in front of the French barracks in the district of Wedding took his job very seriously. Nothing escaped his vigilance, making it impossible for me to slip onto the grounds. For my first 'recruiting mission' I had chosen the French barracks, which were located near what is Tegel airport today. The British barracks were in Gatow, part of Spandau, which inconveniently lay further from the Wall. I could always still try that garrison if things did not work out with the French. I had decided to approach the Americans last.

The French military compound was vast. The General Göring infantry regiment had been quartered there under the Nazis. After the end of the war, the French moved in and named the barracks 'Quartier Napoléon'. In 1995 the compound was renamed as the Julius Leber Barracks, after the resistance fighter.

Now or never! A delivery truck had just pulled up to the entrance, and the driver was exchanging a few words with the soldier standing guard. The moment offered a good opportunity to slip by unseen on the other side of the vehicle. In an instant I was inside the compound; the guard had noticed nothing. I quickly tried to gain an overview of the grounds. My goal was to reach the mess hall because I imagined the soldiers would be hungry around noon and would be heading there in droves. A place where conversation is apt to start. I soon found out where it was. I needed only to follow the smell of fried liver and lentils.

But when I entered the mess hall, I realised I'd made a foolish mistake that I was unable to correct. If only I had informed myself about the various uniforms. Which insignia stood for which rank? To whom did I have to turn in order to talk about our mission? Why hadn't I thought of it earlier? Perhaps because I had absolutely no clue about military matters, much less about French uniforms. The physical examination in Karlsruhe in November 1963 had determined my fitness for duty, but, to my satisfaction, I had received a deferral because I was already enrolled at university. Sneaking into the barracks may have been daring, but more than anything it had been plain naïve. Unfortunately, I did not realise it until that very minute.

The mess hall was jam-packed. I joined the line and picked up a plate – and though I was not wearing a uniform, no one gave me a second look. French soldiers and the German civilians employed by the French army used the same mess hall, so no odd glances came my way. I chose an empty seat next to a Frenchman wearing quite an impressive uniform. My plan was to tell him a pitiful story: my family was in the East, the building of the Wall had separated us and was absolutely dreadful for us all, we'd do anything to reunite, so could he help us?

The French soldier sitting at the table with me was, unfortunately, an officer. I did not manage to lay my tearful tale before him in any great detail. He had quickly recognised that I did not belong there.

'Leave everything on your tray and leave the barracks immediately,' he barked at me in French. 'Otherwise I'll have to summon the military police. You have no business being here.'

Startled, I hurried out with my tail between my legs. I was disappointed but by no means discouraged. The officer had only done his duty. And there were still the American and British barracks. Things rarely work out the first time, I thought, trying to calm myself as I stole away.

Despite better preparation, I fared no better on my subsequent attempts. I did not even set foot on the British compound. They intercepted me before I got that far.

'I ... I'd like...'

The soldier on duty cut me off brusquely. 'Show me your ID,' he snapped.

'I...'

A steely look made me creep away at once. The Americans detained me without hesitation for a couple of hours in their headquarters on Clayallee in Dahlem. Two officers questioned me.

'Why did you want to come into our barracks?'

I decided to tell the truth.

'With your help I would like to bring people from the East into the West – to freedom.' The bit about freedom, in my experience, always went down well with the Americans.

'Is that really your motive?' The Americans eyed me in amazement.

'Yes,' I replied simply, trying to look as convincing as possible.

'You can forget it,' came the sobering answer. But what they really wanted to say was written on their faces. Is this guy serious? He's totally naïve!

And they were right. I may have had a good idea, but instead of proceeding carefully, for example, by approaching the soldiers privately in a bar when they were off duty, I had marched straight into the lions' den. Thinking things through was different.

Later, I wondered whether someone else had come up with a similar idea. I could well imagine that the Americans would help in principle, for instance, if a spy from their own ranks were to ask for support. But spies were a different matter. And maybe help would be forthcoming in order to get a scientist out of the East. But that, too, was something quite different. How could I, as a German escape helper, seriously expect such assistance?

Naturally, Wolfgang and I were disappointed about the failure of my attempts at making contact, and I felt guilty. I kept going to the border, this time alone, getting up close to the 'enemy' in the hope that something innovative would finally occur to me. More than ninety per cent of the tunnels had failed, the percentage of all escape attempts that had failed was even higher. I therefore had to come up with a really good idea. And there were no limits on imagination. The idea with the military had not been bad, but I had bungled it. A new plan was urgently needed. Giving up was not an option for me; I hadn't even properly started yet. Quite the contrary, the desire to move ahead had only intensified because of my own failure so far.

Fuchs did not allow setbacks to discourage him for long. True to form, he was soon radiating his characteristic optimism again.

And because we had not lost our courage, we had a brilliant idea not long after the misadventure at the barracks. It suddenly popped up, and I don't know which of us formulated it first. 'A diplomat! That's the answer! We have to find a diplomat in East Berlin who is not subject to checks or arrest!'

We had often discussed which persons in which vehicles were not checked by the border guards. Aside from the Allied soldiers, there were only the diplomats. A car with diplomatic number plates - that was the solution!

But how were we supposed to approach a diplomat? The options were not exactly plentiful. The GDR was diplomatically isolated from most of the world and was recognised only by the members of COMECON, led by the Soviet Union. Some leftist African and Arab states also recognised it. But other diplomatic relations did not exist.

This situation was essentially the result of West Germany's so-called Hallstein Doctrine, a 1955 foreign policy guideline that was intended to isolate the GDR. If a country established diplomatic relations with the German Democratic Republic, the Federal Republic of Germany regarded the move as an 'unfriendly act' and retaliated by breaking off diplomatic relations. The Hallstein Doctrine was not abandoned until 1969 under West Germany's social-liberal coalition government led by Willy Brandt. Until then it had very successfully prevented East Germany – unlike West Germany – from developing into an internationally recognised country with a host of economic relations. Much of the GDR's industrial production was already divested by the Soviet Union, making it much more attractive for many Asian and African countries, as well as America, to abide by this doctrine and to establish official relations with the FRG. Moreover, the FRG, the country of the economic miracle, could afford development and economic aid, whereas the GDR could only offer limited assistance and then only in consultation with the USSR.

'It's enough if one country co-operates with us,' said Wolfgang, who was instantly fired up at the idea of winning over an accredited diplomat. 'I'll listen around. I could imagine that one or the other could be tempted.'

I forgot to add, 'With what?'

Now things began to move. On a cold day in early February 1966, Fuchs led me to a Syrian carpet dealer whose shop was located on the northern side of the Kurfürstendamm – or Ku'damm for short – not far from Olivaer Platz. Women in fur coats hurried about on the grand boulevard, probably on their way to the nearest café, possibly the Café Kranzler further along. It was still too early for theatres and cinemas. The glamorous world of West Berlin bohemian life did not stir until a later hour. I marvelled at the glass display cases that lined both sides of Ku'damm. They dated back to a 1936 Olympic Games initiative by the National Socialists to bring sophistication and a metropolitan flair to the street. Now the displays were part of the 'showcase of the West'. I was impressed most by the elegant and magnificent late-nineteenth-century Wilhelminian buildings with their lofty entrance portals and halls. In 1963 John F. Kennedy rode down this street together with Willy Brandt, at that time Governing Mayor of West Berlin, and West Germany's Federal Chancellor Konrad Adenauer. It was a kind of triumphal procession for the American president.

I never learned who had set up the contact with the carpet dealer, but it did not really interest me. Fuchs had no doubt ensured that the contact would help us make progress. Efficiency was one of his outstanding traits.

'I'm Fatso,' said the carpet dealer by way of introduction. 'Feel free to call me that. Nobody is able to pronounce my Arabic name anyway. It's also better if it doesn't become generally known.'

'Another Fatso,' I thought, remembering our corpulent bartender; this man, too, was known by that nickname for a reason. He was quite well upholstered and fairly tall. I estimated him to be about forty years old. Heavy horn-rimmed glasses defined his face; his hair was black and seemed slightly greasy.

'We've heard that you have contact to a diplomat who represents your country in East Berlin?' asked Wolfgang cautiously after a few trivial words had been exchanged about carpet trading and we had been served terribly sweet tea by the bespectacled man. He was a heavy smoker. As soon as he had smoked one of his Arabic cigarettes, he would promptly light the next one. Whilst doing so, you couldn't help but notice his fingers, bejewelled with expensive rings set with sparkling stones of many colours.

Fatso nodded vigorously. 'Yes, I have superb connections in my homeland.' He meant the Baath Party, which in 1963 had taken over power in Syria under Hafiz al-Assad, the father of today's President Baschar a-Assad, and which considered the USSR and its so-called democratic centralism as a model. Everything was organised along strictly hierarchical lines as defined by the party. At that time Syria was already a police state whose competing intelligence apparatuses kept the population under control.

'Perhaps you have not quite understood me,' said Fuchs, who was leading the conversation. 'We need an East Berlin diplomat who is not subject to searches when driving a car bearing GDR-issued diplomatic number plates through the border at Checkpoint Charlie into West Berlin.'

'I *have* understood you correctly,' Fatso replied a bit condescendingly and shouted something in Arabic into an adjoining room. We were presently joined by a slender man, perhaps in his mid-thirties, with similarly pitch-black hair, just less greasy. He had a dark complexion, full, pronounced lips, and a very prominent nose.

'This is Kamal Hamdi, Consul of the Syrian Arab Republic in East Berlin,' said the carpet dealer, introducing his compatriot.

What a surprise! We had not expected to be introduced to a real-live diplomat so promptly. The consul said nothing and merely smiled in a friendly manner. He left the talking to Fatso. 'However, there is a little problem,' Fatso explained. 'Unfortunately, my friend has no car. Our government has not assigned him one. And his salary is so small that he cannot afford one.'

So that was the consul's motive for engaging in such a risky operation. As a poorly paid Syrian diplomat without a car, he wanted to improve his status. To this day I do not know how much he received for his services. I assume, however, that he did not earn badly, and fairly regularly at that. Of course, Fuchs knew what sums were involved, but I never asked him.

'Then I'll arrange a car for your friend,' Fuchs assured. 'That shouldn't be an obstacle.'

I was amazed to hear how swiftly Wolfgang had an answer to the problem. Did he have that much money? But as with the diplomat's pay, I did not wish to dwell on the matter. Otherwise, I might have had my doubts, after all. I was glad that everything was settled so quickly and that the meeting had ended successfully.

'Well, we can start soon,' said Wolfgang as we stepped out onto Kurfürstendamm again. He rubbed his hands as though he had negotiated the deal of his life. 'Or do you think he'll back out?'

'I rather had the impression that he'd love to get behind the steering wheel immediately,' I observed.

We ambled together along Ku'damm towards the Memorial Church, each of us mulling over his own thoughts. Shortly before the church, we parted.

'You'll be hearing from me soon,' Fuchs called out as he left.

And I did.

Wolfgang procured a white Mercedes 220 for the Syrian Consul. If you're going to do something, you might as well do it properly. It was a used car, but even that cost more than I estimated Wolfgang to have. Today I think that those Berlin CDU sources paid for the Mercedes, though I cannot prove it. However, Wolfgang repeatedly mentioned his good contacts to the Berlin Christian Democrats. Their interest seemed plausible to me because they did not favour the policy of rapprochement pursued by the Berlin SPD and later, the federal government. The local Christian Democrats may have agreed to pay the costs for converting the car as well. The boot of the Mercedes was not designed to accommodate two or even three people, so it was necessary to reinforce the rear suspension in order to camouflage the car's additional hidden load ranging from 150 to 200 kilograms – up to 440 extra pounds.

The alteration was carried out in a workshop run by one of Manfred's acquaintances. The vehicle then had to be given diplomatic registration plates in East Berlin. As I remember, Kamal Hamdi's deputy, who was informed of the scheme, took care of that step on the consul's behalf. He also had the Daimler registered as an official car in East Berlin. It was then mounted with the diplomatic corps registration plate that guaranteed immunity. The Corps Diplomatique (CD) registration number was 1471; the official registration plates read IU 02-36. After the registration of the car, Wolfgang and I met with Kamal Hamdi to inspect everything. I noticed that the latter spoke only broken German. Perhaps that was not a bad thing, in case the NVA border guards were to ask him any questions.

Things were gradually getting serious. Wolfgang stated point-blank, 'You handle the diplomat.'

'Does that make sense?' I inquired sceptically.

'It makes more than good sense,' Wolfgang stressed. 'You've been in on this affair from the outset. You know all the people, and I don't know anyone who fits the bill better than you.'

Fuchs had a certain talent for sweeping a person along.

'Besides,' he continued, 'you already have a little experience, which I can't count on with many others.'

I looked at him insistently. 'Isn't it rather that you simply don't have anyone else on hand at the moment?'

Somehow, I had hit the nail on the head. Many former helpers had meanwhile withdrawn. He arched his eyebrows.

'Well, that's more or less true.'

'You're really under pressure, aren't you?' I persisted.

'And how,' Wolfgang sighed. 'And the list of people who want out is getting longer and longer.'

I threw Wolfgang a worried look. He seemed very strained, but I still had so many unanswered questions. How and where was I to meet with the escapees? How was I to deliver them to the diplomat? Who would determine the pick-up points? How would I stow the people quickly in the boot of the car? How was I to make sure that the driver and the escapees would not recognise each other? How would the trip to the checkpoint proceed?

Wolfgang seemed to have guessed what I was thinking. 'You have to prepare everything in detail,' he said. 'You have sole responsibility for the East. Isn't that what you wanted? More self-initiative?'

I gulped involuntarily. Sole responsibility for the East – that didn't sound like 'somewhat more' responsibility but rather like a damned lot of responsibility.

'Doesn't it actually violate your credo that we all should know as little as possible?' I ventured tentatively.

'Yes, but there's no other way in this case. The matter lies in your hands now.' Wolfgang looked at me reassuringly. 'And don't forget to clarify the handover points. Do that long before things begin to happen.'

'And how am I to find them?'

'Quite simple. You'll presumably have to enter East Berlin repeatedly and explore the terrain. I can't do it; I'd be arrested immediately. The Stasi knows exactly who I am.'

'Can't you nevertheless still give me a few tips? You know your way around much better in East Berlin.' I looked at Wolfgang expectantly.

After reflecting briefly, he said, 'It's important that you feel at ease in the area. Check very closely beforehand how best to get in and out. And another thing: you should not accompany the escapees every step of the way. Always only intermittently. Have them occasionally walk alone to check whether they're being watched. And remember to use a different place for each escape. You mustn't fall into a routine. You mustn't allow a pattern to emerge, or the Stasi will have easy pickings.'

I had already considered all of this. Wolfgang was right; it was important that I appear to be at home in East Berlin. That applied not only to me but to the escapees as well. They might never have been in the city before. Maybe they were from Jena, Dresden, or Leipzig. No easy task for any of the people involved.

Right after my exchange with Wolfgang, I bought an East Berlin city map and looked at a few of the outskirts that

I guessed could come into question. In the north-east, Marzahn seemed suitable; in the south-east, the environs of Müggelsee, a large recreational lake. Both areas were logistically easy for Kamal Hamdi to find by car. A handover in the centre of the city was out of the question. There were too many windows behind which too many eyes could observe what we were doing. The fewer the people, the smaller the danger of being discovered. And that meant seeking out open ground. But there was a snag with that, too. A white Mercedes parked without a reason in the middle of nowhere would stand out, of course. Basically, the chosen place had to be all but deserted – no people, no cars. And that in a major city.

Next, I thought about the logistics of delivering the escapees. Visual signals from my small torch and from Kamal Hamdi's headlights seemed a sensible way to communicate. I worked out a system: three short flashes to the other party would mean the presence of extreme danger; one short, one long, then another short flash would mean all OK; and three long beams at five-second intervals would mean that the operation had to be broken off. I passed this code to Wolfgang. Just in case it was not yet dark enough for such communication at the time of the handover, I had agreed on corresponding arm gestures.

'Try to work in the dark if at all possible,' Wolfgang had advised me.

That was not a problem now in spring. But in summer, darkness wouldn't fall until late, and I had to be back in the West before my day visa expired at midnight.

Fuchs had ready advice: 'If it should get too tight, just get into the car and sit down next to the Syrian. He can then drop you off at the nearest tram or bus stop.'

That sounded like a useful suggestion. But yet another problem had to be solved: the number plates on the front and back of the car. The sequence of numbers and letters had to remain unknown to the escapees so that they could not divulge it even if questioned. Hamdi was therefore instructed to shine his full beam headlights after seeing my signal that the coast was clear. I was responsible for the rear plate. Just before 'loading' the car, I would have to put a little distance between me and the escapees. As the car approached, I would have them face away from the car so that I could open the boot unobserved. With the lid open, no one could read the rear registration plate. After the car's full beam headlights were turned on, the driver would cover his face with a scarf or a hat so that he, too, was not seen by the escapees.

I had decided to meet the escapees in the centre of town and to do the handover in the outskirts. That seemed the safest to me. I thought Friedrichstrasse and Alexanderplatz were suitable places, busy and impossible to miss. As had been the case with my courier assignments, I had to think up a new message for each meeting, some code word or phrase by which we could identify each other. Innocuous sentences such as 'I'm glad to see you again.' were suitable. None were to be used more than once, however, so I had to come up with an entire list. In my reckoning, Wolfgang would then send the messages by courier. Now I knew what 'Call your grandmother' could have meant.

'There is still something we have to discuss,' I told Wolfgang when we met up once again at Fatso's. 'I have to go back to Bonn. And isn't it a little crazy to do everything from there – all the time it takes, all the costs?'

'If you're thinking of withdrawing, forget it. You've already prepared so much. You can't leave me hanging.'

He was right. I could not leave him in the lurch. I couldn't bring myself to do that. Most of all, I did not want to quit just before the finishing line. My two semesters in Berlin were coming to an end, and I wanted finally to complete my law degree in Bonn. In Berlin I was in the middle of completing my intermediate degree in political economics and was focusing fairly hard on it. There were special reasons for that. My father, sorely disappointed that I did not want to follow in his footsteps as an engineer, had accused me of ducking a hard subject like maths. I found that unfair and wanted to prove him wrong by taking exams in a subject like political economics, which required a good deal of maths. I succeeded. In Bonn I had registered for a course preparing for the law exams. It was led by a nationally renowned tutor, Dr Schneider. He excelled at taking the vast legal knowledge required and reducing it to the essentials.

'Well, then go and do your exams on the Rhine,' said Wolfgang after I had told him that I nevertheless wanted to stay on. 'I am sure we'll manage!'

'And the costs of the flights'?

'You'll be reimbursed, of course.'

This was the only instance in which I ever talked with Wolfgang about money. But, naturally, it had to come from somewhere. I could not imagine that the consul was the only one to receive an attractive sum for his contribution to the escapes. I continued to consider Fuchs as basically selfless, and even if he did receive some money from friends or dependents of the people prepared to escape, it seemed fair to me because his involvement was unlikely to have left him much time to pursue normal paid work. He had to live and support his family from these donations alone.

'Still, you ought to find a substitute for me. It could always happen that I won't get back to Berlin in time.' I had urged that several times already.

'Yeah, yeah,' Wolfgang waved dismissively. 'I have someone in mind already. But I'd like you to have a look at him with me first.'

'Doesn't that contradict your conspiratorial rules again? Shouldn't I be in the dark about who else is working with you? Wouldn't that also be better for the new person, too, not to meet me?'

Fuchs shrugged. 'Please, Volker. I'd like you to help me make the right choice.'

I did not disagree further. I was somehow in awe that Fuchs really wanted to have my opinion. I could no longer avoid it.

That evening we met Heiko Neumann in a pub. It was not at Fatso's but a place frequented only by travellers passing through the railway station at Zoologischer Garten. We each had a currywurst and a beer. Heiko was of medium height, had a rather slight build and brown hair, and seemed rather pale to me. A nondescript type.

'Are you a student?' asked Wolfgang, dragging a slice of sausage through the red curry sauce. 'You told me once already, I think, but I just want to make sure I remember correctly.' Fuchs recruited all his people from the universities. That made perfect sense because anyone with a job and a family simply could not run the risk of being exposed as an escape helper.

'Yes,' Heiko Neumann confirmed. 'I'm in my eighth semester of philosophy.'

'And why would you like to get involved?' I asked.

Neumann regarded us solemnly, and then he said, 'If we don't help other people living in a system they can't accept, then humanity is abandoned: we forsake our humanness and become animals.' Only a philosophy student could put it like that. Neumann carried on quite a while about his humanitarian duty to help. Money did not seem to play a role for him, either. At least he did not ask what he would earn on the operations.

After he had left, Fuchs and I remained seated for a second glass of beer.

'What do you think of our young humanist?' smirked Fuchs. I side-stepped the question.

'Well, maybe it would work. But I don't know him well enough. Just try to find out more about his background. It's your decision!'

'You don't sound all that convinced. Why so sceptical?'

'Hard to say. He seemed pretty insecure to me. And the bit about being like animals and humans, well, I found it much too abstract.'

'I had the same feeling, but people like you and Manfred don't come along every day.'

I would have liked Manfred at my side. But he did not want to continue. He said he felt drained, so drained that he was not progressing with his studies anymore. That was what had been depressing him when I discovered him in the *Stern* article during my visit. 'Go to Heidelberg,' I advised him. 'Go to my fraternity, where you might make new friends. But especially, you'll get some rest. Heidelberg is manageable, less stressful than Berlin.' After a bit of friendly persuasion he really did continue his medical studies in Heidelberg. Not long afterwards he passed his exams.

'Let's simply hope Heiko is a good choice,' I told Fuchs, somewhat preoccupied.

A few days later I was driving to Bonn in my trusty, jam-packed VW – this time without getting lost.

THE FIRST ESCAPE

Finally it came. The long-awaited yet dreaded telephone call. 'Volker, tomorrow you board the plane. It's on.' Wolfgang gave no details. It was said that conversations between West Germany and West Berlin could not be intercepted by the GDR but we didn't count on it. It was better to play safe.

After confirming the call with a straightforward 'yes,' I hung up. My pulse instantly began to quicken, my heart hammering loudly in my chest. It was my first proper deployment, and I was incredibly nervous. Over time I developed more routine, but even then the agitation never completely subsided.

In the morning I would be heading to Berlin. I would miss out on the crash course with Dr Schneider as well as some university lectures and tutorials. Suddenly I became aware of what I was expecting of myself. It would not be easy to study for exams as well as help people escape. Nonetheless, my thirst for adventure remained unabated. And my sense of justice was undimmed. In fact, the time in Berlin had only reinforced it.

The next morning I made my way to the Cologne-Wahn airport. At that time, only the three airlines of the western Allies – Air France, Pan Am, and British European Airways – were permitted to land in West Berlin, and it was only from them that I could purchase tickets. It was not possible to board a Lufthansa plane to Berlin. The airline was not allowed to resume flights to Berlin until after Germany's re-unification. On the day of my first escape operation, I flew with the British airline.

About an hour later, towards noon, I landed at Tempelhof airport. I had a meal at a place near the border, for I did not reckon on being able to get something to eat again anytime soon. Besides, hunger would only have distracted me, and I could not afford any lapses of concentration. Fuchs kept me company during lunch, but the real purpose of the meeting was to give me instructions.

'OK, the people already know what's going to happen,' he said. 'There are two of them. Meet them next to Ganymed.' The restaurant on Schiffbauerdamm, near Friedrichstrasse, was as popular with the Stasi as it had been some time earlier with Bertolt Brecht and Helene Weigel. The famous Berliner Ensemble theatre, where the two artists had worked, lay directly behind it.

'And how will they recognise me?' I poked nervously at my fries. The agitation had reduced my appetite, a new phenomenon for me.

'The courier has described you to them. With your height, you won't be overlooked.' (I'm over 6 foot 2.) Wolfgang hungrily ate his meatballs smothered in mustard along with the ample serving of fries he too had ordered.

'And how do I recognise them? There's a lot happening on Schiffbauerdamm.'

'One of the two will be holding a standard technical reference book under his arm. He's an engineer. Whatever is used to identify them has to be acceptable in the eyes of the escapees. They have to feel at ease. It will therefore be different each time. A city map, a flower, or whatever.'

Wolfgang dabbed his mouth with his white paper napkin and leaned back, visibly contented. Apart from a few smudges of mustard his plate was completely empty. I had finished only half of mine.

'Volker, listen to me. Flexibility is the most important thing in what we do. If we're not flexible, we'll be found out very quickly.'

'Is there anything else I need to know about the two of them?' I enquired, trying to keep calm.

'The less you know, the better. But the other person is a young woman. The two are not a couple, though,' Wolfgang added, emphasising the final sentence. After a brief pause, he added: 'Good luck!' Reaching over the table, he patted me on the back. 'I'll pay the bill.'

I rose from my seat, put on my coat, and buttoned it all the way to the collar – it was a cool April day. Lingering for a moment outside of the restaurant, I took a deep breath. Two people, I thought. Well then, get going. On the way it occurred to me that Wolfgang had seemed a little uneasy when he mentioned the young woman. Did he perhaps know her? Only years later did I learn that she was to become Wolfgang's second wife. No wonder he was especially nervous about this escape.

I had meanwhile become quite familiar with the border crossing at Friedrichstrasse, so I had chosen it for my first operation. And Ganymed was only about five minutes away from there. Three additional checkpoints were also available to

West Germans: Heinrich Heine Strasse, Bornholmer Strasse, and Invalidenstrasse. In keeping with the principle of staying flexible, I used all four border crossings over the weeks and months. Invalidenstrasse was the least advantageous geographically speaking, so I did not use it often. A dramatic escape attempt had failed there in May 1963, when twelve men and women in a bus tried to crash through the barriers. The guards opened fire and the bus came to a halt in a narrow opening in the Wall just short of the border. The driver and several would-be escapees were seriously wounded – and immediately arrested, of course.

As I approached the border installation, I knew what awaited me there: a musty odour and austere border officers scrutinising me as though they wanted to arrest me on the spot. That was for show. I needn't worry. I had not yet accompanied an escapee to the Syrian's Mercedes. Luckily, they could not read minds, though some of them would all too gladly have done so. Everything went smoothly. My day visa received its reference number and stamp. As always, the hammer and sickle stood out in glaring tomato red. After pushing aside the thick dark felt curtain that shielded the open door from the cold wind, I could already smell the East Berlin air.

I ambled as nonchalantly as possible up Schiffbauerdamm and soon recognised the pair by the giant engineering book tucked under the arm of a man in his late twenties. Both of them appeared to be attentively studying the menu posted by the door of the restaurant. To an onlooker they really seemed to be carefully considering whether they liked what was on offer.

From time to time the woman, who was pretty, dark-haired, and well-groomed, smiled as though she were looking forward to the evening out with the man beside her. The two of them credibly appeared to be lovers. That was good.

'An outstanding standard reference work,' I said, stopping next to them and pointing to the thick book. That was the code Wolfgang had given me.

The man and the woman nodded almost simultaneously. Their eyes twitched nervously; they were at least as agitated as I was – except that my inner disquiet had to be masked at all costs. The escapees were supposed to feel secure. An air of panic would only have jeopardised the operation.

'Alex. Haus des Lehrers. 3 pm.' I said.

More nodding. Wolfgang's messenger had informed both of them that we would not constantly remain together on this day, that for their own safety they had to manage part of the way themselves. Not knowing how well the two knew their way around in Berlin, I had chosen Alexanderplatz. Anyone would eventually find it. We parted in silence, I in one direction, the 'couple' in the other. Several routes led to Alex from here. The 'Haus des Lehrers', the first high-rise on Alexanderplatz, was impossible to miss.

There was a very special chemistry between us from the outset. I tried to grasp it, but that was difficult. We were mutual strangers, yet these two people were now dependent on me. There was something eerie about such an encounter. My hands were clammy, and I repeatedly needed to swallow because sheer anxiety about doing something 'wrong' had made me forget to breathe.

The 'lovers' had arrived at the appointed place a bit earlier, but I had intended that. All the better to check whether they were being observed. I saw nothing, though. Nothing that unsettled me. After the two had noticed me, we walked our separate ways to a tram stop. They boarded at the front; I, at the rear.

'Leave the tram when I nod to you,' I had whispered to the couple beforehand when we had met up at the Haus des Lehrers. 'It will take a while, shortly before the last stop. Try to converse with each other normally. Don't look over to me until the tram has travelled at least fifteen stops.

The route took us through the heavily damaged centre of East Berlin, heading southeast. As agreed, I nodded to them and we left the eggshell-coloured carriages, known as Reko-trams to East Germans. We were now in the vicinity of Müggelsee. No one disembarked with us, although a few passengers still remained in the carriage. The experience was similar on each of the several occasions I had travelled this part of the route. The place was perfect for our plan.

We walked along the edge of an unploughed field. We could have spoken to each other now, sharing our respective motives. But we did not. Our tongues were tied. Constant fear lurked. What if we were being watched after all? Anxiety led us to imagine spies crouching in the field. The thought ocurred to me that all I knew about the man was that he was an engineer. These people were total strangers to me, and for them I was now taking all these risks upon myself. But the escapees, too, were taking enormous risks: leaving behind everything they had, not just things but friends, family, and relying solely on me! It was a strange thought, but I could not deny feeling a certain surge of adrenalin. The two people could depend only on the hope that I understood the personal distress that had moved them to flee their homeland. Once again, I became aware that they had to trust me unconditionally without knowing me. I imagined that to be very hard, for they had no basis for this trust. It was like jumping into cold water, for both sides.

Darkness had meanwhile fallen, but that did not help the two people with me to feel safer. The closer we came to the agreed meeting point for transfer to the car, the more nervous they became. Their fear was palpable, and I had trouble not allowing it to infect me as well. I silently cautioned myself against losing my nerve. Stay calm, don't look at your watch too often.

Finally, I saw the car slowing approaching us in the distance. The Syrian had noticed us too and signalled with his headlights as agreed. Everything OK. I walked a distance ahead. Suddenly, the young woman behind me said, 'I have to pee.'

I looked at her in disbelief. 'I'm sorry,' I replied. 'But now's not the time.'

'It's really urgent,' she insisted.

'Not now. You have to hold out.'

'I can't.'

Although I was really very sorry, I did not give in. I had no choice. She could not simply disappear here into the bushes at the edge of the path. During this time, the man could have leisurely studied the Daimler and its driver. I had to prevent that at all cost. 'Pull yourself together. In about thirty minutes you'll be in West Berlin with or without a full bladder.' No one had told me how to respond to such situations.

I quickly opened the boot. The man climbed in first because of the car's axle load. The heavier person must always lie at the back of the boot; the lighter person, at the front. With only a short drive involved, we had not thought in detail about ensuring sufficient oxygen. I presumed, however, that Wolfgang had tested it. If complications were to arise, the escapees could knock. All these things seemed plausible to me, and I trusted Wolfgang's caution. But I suddenly no longer felt prepared. Innumerable questions shot through my mind. Did the Syrian have a car jack with him? The thought occurred to me as I closed the boot. A spare tyre? I had not inspected the boot. Of course, every Mercedes had the appropriate equipment in case the car had a flat tyre, but would Kamal Hamdi know how to use it? Fortunately, the car never had any trouble, not once.

I nodded to the Syrian who then started the engine. The car rolled away towards Checkpoint Charlie, the checkpoint for military personnel, foreigners, and diplomats. I returned to Friedrichstrasse, shaken but trying to keep my composure. At the Friedrichstrasse checkpoint I presented my ID and submitted my day pass. All with no problem.

Done. I was in the West again. At first, I could not believe that everything had gone so smoothly. I was still charged up. Where to now? Of course, to Fatso's. Wolfgang wanted to wait for me there. When I entered, I could already see in his face that the escape must have succeeded.

'They're both exhilarated,' he said, slapping me on the back. 'Well done, Volker!'

I felt incredible relief swell inside me. So all the effort had paid off. No NVA border guard had suspected anything. They had simply waved Kamal through. We had to drink a toast to that! Yes, that really was something, wasn't it? I was pretty proud of myself. Cheers, Rudi Dutschke. You are undoubtedly still brandishing your megaphone!

I no longer remember where I slept that night. I moved from place to place often in the months thereafter, staying at Joachim's or Ulrich's, sometimes at Wolfgang's, sometimes at a fraternity, sometimes at Gudrun's. It was important to avoid routine in this regard as well. If I had not arranged to see Fuchs, I would call him as soon as I returned to West Berlin in order to hear whether everything had gone well. Wolfgang and his people always knew the outcome much sooner than I did. After the escapees had successfully crossed the border, he would drop them off in an interior courtyard in Steglitz after the businesses there had closed for the night. I was never present for that final step.

The next morning, I took the first flight back to Cologne-Wahn. Most of the passengers were civil servants who regularly commuted between Bonn and Berlin with skinny briefcases and grey overcoats. After landing, I climbed into my Volkswagen, stepped on the gas and turned up half an hour late to Dr Schneider's crash course. The whole time I had not realised how much the operation had strained my nerves. It was not until I was sitting in the seminar room that I noticed I could barely concentrate. I tried with all my strength to follow Dr Schneider's words, but my mind kept wandering to quite different and very dramatic scenes: NVA border guards opening the boot of a car only to discover two corpses... My pulse dropped and I broke out in a cold sweat. This mental drama faded somewhat over time, but focusing on a lecture in a totally different part of the country after having pulled off a heady escape operation was a challenge I had evidently underestimated.

SOMEBODY HAS TO KNOW

'I couldn't reach you all day last Friday. We had a date!' Barbara glared at me reproachfully. I could well understand her anger – Fuchs had asked me to come to Berlin at short notice, and I had not been able to tell my girlfriend in time that Friday evening would fall through. She was a trainee teacher. We had been together for several weeks, and I had not breathed a word of my Berlin existence. As Wolfgang had insisted, 'No one, do you understand, no one must know. That's clear to you, isn't it?' I had given my solemn promise to remain as silent as the grave. It was a matter of honour to me. What a question! Secrecy was the cardinal rule, particularly since I had no desire to involve anyone else.

I looked at Barbara remorsefully and took her hand. 'I'm so sorry, really. I had to go home, a family affair. My mother was very upset and called me,' I lied. I could not have used some university obligation as a pretext; Barbara would never have believed, much less accepted it, but asserting that I urgently needed to go home for my mother's sake was not something she could object to.

'I understand. Is someone sick? It wasn't serious, was it?' she asked in a voice both startled and sympathetic.

'No, not at all, but it concerned my studies again. My father had to vent his anger at me.' It was not easy for me to lie. I was ashamed but had no other choice. If I had told Barbara about my adventures, she would doubtless have turned as white as a sheet. She came from a well-to-do Hamburg family, the daughter of a shipping merchant. We were very serious about each other, and although I liked her a lot, I was not yet mature enough for a long-term relationship. Besides, without a degree and my own income, I would have felt like an imposter. That is also why we had not moved in together. I lived in a room near the law department; she had a room in the basement of a villa on the picturesque banks of the Rhine.

Nor was my family to know anything about my secret. My mother would have been so worried about me that she would not have had a moment's peace. Of her four children, I was her favourite, as my siblings sometimes remarked with a mixture of envy and irony. She helped me become a strong person and gave me self-confidence. Her great love and self-sacrifice for her children had been highly formative for me. My father's primary response would probably have been to see his suspicion confirmed that I never wanted to grow up. He was intensely sceptical of my thirst for adventure.

'The problems with your father never seem to end, do they?' sighed Barbara as she drew me close to her. The fact that I had stood her up was already forgotten. I silently justified myself by recalling that I was not allowed to endanger the escape operations in any way and must not implicate my friends and family. As I said good-bye to Barbara the next morning, she said with a wink, 'Next time maybe you'll manage to let me know beforehand.'

'I'll try.' But deep down I knew the dilemma could easily recur.

I increasingly felt the immense pressure weighing on me. The more people I brought over the border, the greater the need became to confide in someone. But in whom? It had to be someone not emotionally involved yet well-disposed to me and able to help in an emergency. I pondered over the question for a long time. At last someone came to mind. A senior fraternity brother, traditionally referred to with the honorific title *Alter Herr*, meaning Senior Gentleman. His name was Hanns Martin Schleyer. Schleyer had been on the board of directors of Daimler-Benz since 1963. He was a man of courage and fortitude, both professionally and privately. He also knew the art of confidentiality – an essential trait for an industrial negotiator in wage disputes. We liked each other. His son, Hanns-Eberhard, also a member of Suevia in Heidelberg, was studying law, as was I. We were friends. In addition, the parents of my first great love were friends of Hanns Martin and his wife. Schleyer presumably knew more about me than about the other members of our fraternity. My idea was that, by virtue of his position, he was probably the only person with a prospect of handling matters if something should go wrong. I had made up my mind. However, I did not want to tell Fuchs about it for the time being.

Our fraternity traditionally held its early spring semester gathering in mid-April. This recruitment event provided a good opportunity for me to approach Schleyer. All the members met in our building's *Kneipsaal*, a grand, wood-panelled beer hall with stained-glass windows. The junior members sat on one side of the long, dark, wooden tables; the *Alte Herren* opposite them. The official part of the evening, enlivened by many toasts and student songs, lasted about an hour, after which members usually stayed on until late to socialise in the convivial atmosphere. That was my chance. I waited for an appropriate moment when Schleyer was not engaged in conversation, and without further ado, addressed him directly.

'Alter Herr Schleyer,' I began. It was customary to address a senior fraternity brother in this manner even though he was only 51 and not old at all. 'Could we talk outside briefly? Alone? It's very important to me.'

Schleyer looked at me searchingly, somewhat surprised, then merely said, 'Let's go to the foyer,' and rose from his chair. I was amazed that he asked no questions. We found a secluded corner, and without mincing my words I began. 'I would like you to know about something. You are the only one I am telling this, and I ask you to keep it strictly confidential.' I paused and took a deep breath. 'I'm involved in helping people escape across the border in Berlin. Everything has gone well so far.' I gave no details.

Schleyer gave me a penetrating look. He was not a fearful man, in fact more of a daredevil. As a student he had duelled with sabre and pistol. I could assume that he would not try to dissuade me from continuing my work as an escape helper. Astonishingly, he said almost nothing to my confession, just 'Good. I've noted it.' I was amazed. I had not reckoned with such a relaxed response. Then a question did come. 'And is something already happening?'

'Yes,' I replied. 'Fourteen people are already here.' It was important to me to be able to present Schleyer with a success story.

'But you do realise that it is not without its dangers?'

'Certainly,' I said. 'And if something actually does go wrong, then I would like you to inform my parents and help them so far as that's possible.'

'That goes without saying.' I could tell he wanted to add something, but then he seemed to change his mind.

'There is something that might tie into your activities. I'll be in touch with you soon.' And with these words he returned to his table and I to mine. I felt greatly relieved. It reassured me that someone trustworthy and influential now had some idea of what I was up to in Berlin. At that time I did not know that he had resigned from the fraternity under the Third Reich because he had not managed to persuade the Heidelberg fraternities to commit themselves to the National Socialist line and its 'comradeship houses'. About a quarter of a century later he succeeded in re-entering the fraternity, though not without stiff resistance. But now he was still an all-round admirable man to me. Only many years later, when I learned of his Nazi past, did my image of him become somewhat tainted. A few days after our encounter at the fraternity, he rang me.

'You could be helpful in a certain matter,' he explained, coming straight to the point.

'What's it about?' I inquired.

'It concerns one of our fraternity brothers, Horst-Peter Hoffmann. His sister Marion is married to an East Berlin doctor named Max Rittersberger. They have three children, and the whole family wants to leave the Zone.'

'Three children?' I swallowed. Fuchs had categorically refused to put children into the boot of a car to transport them across the border.

'Well, they're basically not children any more. The daughter will soon be taking her final secondary school exams, the older son is studying medicine. He's as old as you are. And the younger son is somewhere in between. But what is important for me to know now is how you bring people out?'

'With a diplomatic vehicle,' I answered tersely.

'Aha. Sounds like a relatively safe thing. Do you think you could help this family?'

The time had long past when I could have said no. I did not like the fact that Schleyer had already told me so much about the family, where they lived and what they did. Fuchs had so far never informed me about 'my' escapees, not even their ages. Before each operation I received only a vague description of the person involved. 'I can ask,' I ventured cautiously. 'But...'

'Oh, I just remembered, there's something else,' interrupted Schleyer. 'The family has a little one, a daughter. She's about two years old, I think. You were about to say something...'

Good grief, I thought to myself. It wouldn't be easy to convince Wolfgang, so I just said, 'With so many people, it certainly wouldn't be cheap.'

'How much?' asked Schleyer.

'No idea,' I answered honestly. 'I only know that the diplomat has to be paid, perhaps other helpers or messengers. I don't know any details.'

'Do you receive money for it?'

'No. Not a penny.'

'You do it out of pure idealism?'

'Yes.'

After the pivotal experience with Manfred and the story in *Stern*, I had made a decision. I had often asked myself whether

I could justify my actions. From a purely legal perspective, I was, of course, abetting a commercial escape operation, even if I myself was never paid. This quandary was often on my mind.

'Can you find out the costs?'

'I think so,' I responded.

* * *

Fuchs was anything but enthusiastic. I did manage to convince him that Schleyer was exceedingly tight-lipped, but the fact that the escape involved a toddler really put him off.

'Are you crazy?' he exclaimed after hearing my report. 'A family with three nearly grown children is OK, but a girl as young as that is still almost an infant.' I had actually expected him to be upset about my contact to Schleyer, but nothing of the sort.

'Two years old is not a baby anymore,' I countered.

'Please, don't start splitting hairs.'

'I do admit it's a risk.'

'It's a huge risk, and my list has enough names on it. Besides, some have already been waiting for a long time.'

'Listen,' I said. 'So many of your student helpers are in a duelling fraternity. I know that's strange to you, but you'd do me a great favour by putting this family on your list, and please not at the bottom of it.'

For a long time, Wolfgang said nothing. And then he accepted my request: 'Well, only because you're doing such good work. And we have to think hard about how we're going to do it with the child.'

The most difficult part was dealt with. All I had to do now was find out about the costs of the escape.

'What do people who want to escape from the East pay?'

'Fifteen thousand Deutsche Mark,' replied Fuchs impassively.

'For the six-member family?'

He shook his head. My eyes widened.

'Per person? No matter what age?' I found it a surprisingly large sum.

'Correct. Per person. And there's no reduction for children, in case you want to know.' Everyone costs the same. But the baby goes for free.

'It's not a baby.'

'Whatever. I don't want to earn any money for the kid.'

'You almost sound like you could be generous.'

'The prices are tightly calculated. We simply have a lot of expenses.' Fuchs's voice had turned serious.

'I don't want to know any details. I believe you.'

Seventy-five thousand marks – that was an enormous amount of money then. And I was suddenly sure that a handsome profit was made with such a high sum. By someone. For the first time, a slight shadow fell over my relationship to Wolfgang, but I quickly brushed it aside.

I phoned Schleyer that very evening. 'It will cost a total of seventy-five thousand marks,' I said somewhat haltingly.

His answer came promptly. 'Good, you'll receive the money.'

That was it. The call was over. Schleyer had said not a word about what to me seemed like an exorbitant sum.

Shortly before the operation, the money was brought in a thick, sealed envelope to my student apartment at 35 Bachstrasse in Bonn; not by Schleyer personally but by his chauffeur in his official limousine, a black Mercedes-Benz 600. I suppose he paid some of it out of his own pocket, but I do not know. Maybe one or another fraternity member contributed something. We never spoke about it.

Meanwhile, I had sent a telegram to my fraternity brother in the Palatinate who was hoping that I would bring his sister, brother-in-law and their four children to the West. In the message I requested that he call me on a certain day on a specified number. A few days later he rang. I asked only, 'Still interested?'

'Absolutely.'

There was a problem, however. Clearly, not all six people would fit in the boot of the car. Up to then we had allowed only two persons per trip, but an exception had to be made for a six-member family: two trips, each with three persons.

'Don't we want to make the trip twice in one day for the Rittersbergers?' Fuchs asked me after we had discussed who would go when. 'Then they'll be quickly reunited and wouldn't have to spend a horrible night in suspense.'

'I think it would be too dangerous. We would have to undertake the first tour in broad daylight. Just covering the distances with public transport would be nearly impossible. And what if we were being watched?'

'Do you think that's the case?'

'No.'

'Well then, why the pessimism?'

'I don't want to be pessimistic. I just want to proceed as safely as possible. What will the border officials at Checkpoint Charlie think when the same vehicle drives into West Berlin twice in one day?'

'OK, OK. You're the boss in this thing,' Wolfgang tried to reassure me. 'What do you suggest? How should we tackle it?'

'The three older children first, then the parents with the little girl on the following day.'

I definitely didn't want the parents to flee first. If something were to go wrong, the children, who were still minors, were bound to land in an orphanage. An appalling thought. The risk had to be minimised.

Fortunately, all went well. The three adolescents squeezed into the boot without much problem. And on the next day, even the little girl made no suspicious sounds throughout the trip. It was a wonderful feeling to be able to give my fraternity brother the good news the next day. I dialled Schleyer's home phone number. With infinite relief I told him that everything had turned out well. I also felt good to know he was aware of what I was doing – and might help me someday if things should go wrong.

GIVING THE LEATHER JACKETS
THE SLIP

The number of my East-West crossings grew bigger and bigger. Week after week, we continued bringing people out of East Berlin. I imagined the border guards at the checkpoints keeping tally sheets and then asking with raised eyebrows: why does this fellow Volker Heinz come to East Berlin so often?

But in those days there were no computers, no search functions for screening names. I seldom saw a familiar face when receiving a day visa. And what danger could just one person pose? Vehicles that could be used for escapes were far more interesting, which is why the guards concentrated on them by using small two-wheeled carts equipped with a long iron handle and a mirror to view the underside of the vehicle and the area above the wheels. The boot and passenger spaces were carefully inspected as well. As a pedestrian I could at best carry a few books in my pockets, but certainly not people.

So I brushed my reservations aside. No, I was not being tracked. There was no evident connection between what I was doing and the admittedly frequent trips by the Syrian diplomat in the white

Mercedes. He had many friends in the West, like the carpet dealer on Ku'damm. Not a big deal!

But then something totally unexpected happened. One of the men whom I had helped escape returned to the GDR shortly afterwards. As I later discovered from Stasi files, a love story was involved. He was interrogated for hours after his return, but was unable to reveal much. In hindsight I was proud we had prepared everything so carefully that he could not even identify the registration plate of the get-away car!

Nevertheless, complications arose. Twice I aborted an escape attempt because I feared that I was being shadowed. I could not rationally explain to myself or to Wolfgang why I had suddenly been so sure that I had to break off the operation. But my instinct for dangerous situations had demanded it. It was bad for the escapees, of course, because I couldn't inform them of my decision. I had to leave them to their terrible uncertainty. I simply didn't show up. No explanation whatsoever, and the Syrian waiting for us in vain.

On one of those days, I was absolutely convinced that two men were following me and that their steps accelerated whenever mine did. I began walking faster and faster and eventually broke into a run to shake them off. I had let people down who were counting on me. I felt very weak and totally helpless. I had no way to tell the escapees, Wolfgang, or the Syrian.

It was like being the lead actor in a spy movie. I thought my only chance to elude the men chasing me would be to jump into an approaching train as quickly as possible. Fortunately, an underground station was nearby from where I could travel to the Friedrichstrasse border crossing without having to change lines.

I reached the station's platform completely out of breath and turned around. There could be no doubt. Two men in leather jackets were rushing down the stairs to the platform. A train had pulled in, people were getting off and on. The doors were still open. I quickly stepped in. Made it. The next moment the doors closed. The two men trailing me did not manage to jump into the carriage in time. The train pulled away. My heart was racing and hammering in my chest. At each station I feared the two men would suddenly turn up again. That was hardly possible – how would they be able to catch up so quickly? But fear suddenly made unrealistic scenarios seem very real. And what if they had informed their colleagues?

The Friedrichstrasse station was as crowded as ever. Even if my pursuers were hot on my heels, they would not be able to spot me easily in this throng – that is, if they expected me here in the first place. Did they know what I was up to?

Surrounded by all the people at the station, I felt safer and began to calm down. Without once looking around, I made my way to the border crossing. The officials checked my papers. Everything went without a hitch. I was able to resume my journey without delay and left the S-Bahn at the station on Lehrter Strasse (Lehrter Bahnhof, now Hauptbahnhof).

The terrifying ordeal in the eastern part of the city had not lasted more than twenty minutes, but it had seemed like an eternity. The entire time, I had expected to be arrested at any moment. But now I was suddenly no longer completely sure that I had been under surveillance at all. Maybe it had been nothing but hallucinations, and I had made it all up. Maybe.

The two men had been between thirty and forty years old as I remember, both of them slim and fit – no paper-pushers. One of them had dark-blond hair; the other, black. Their clothing had been unremarkable: light-coloured shirts beneath their leather jackets, dark trousers, and shoes that looked quite trendy by East German standards. I repeatedly told myself that I had only imagined it all, that no one had been shadowing me, that there had been no danger of arrest. How was I to check whether what I had felt was right?

I hurried to Wolfgang in Friedenau as quickly as possible. I was pretty depressed. I had to talk to someone about it.

'Whatever is the matter with you?' asked Wolfgang after opening his apartment door on Fregestrasse. Normally, security precautions dictated that we were never to meet where he lived. But we were amateurs, after all.

Still fairly distraught, I told him the whole story. When I had finished, Wolfgang said, 'Since they didn't catch you at the border, it's unlikely they've identified you.'

'Still, we cannot just ignore the fact that two men were after me,' I interjected. 'Am I a spent force for the escape business now? Do they have me on their radar?'

'There are two options,' said Wolfgang. 'Either you quit, or you do a test run.'

'You mean I should offer myself as a guinea pig?'

Wolfgang countered with a question of his own: 'How else do you want to find out whether you've been observed or not?'

I stared at Wolfgang. 'And what if they arrest me?'

'I can't guarantee it won't happen. But if you don't try it out, you'll never know. And it would really be a pity if we had to do without you.'

'I'll have to think about it.'

'Do. You'll come to the right decision for sure.'

I thought about the situation for a long time and took, from today's perspective, the wrong decision. I had to find out whether anyone in East Berlin really was after us. I cannot explain why I made up my mind that way, but it simply was not my style to leave things unresolved.

'I'm going back in,' I told Wolfgang. 'It sounds incredible. A normal person would find it hard to understand.'

'Well, you are not a normal person. You've taken big risks right from the start. But honestly, what can they prove you've done? Absolutely nothing.'

I nodded pensively. Once again, he had managed to raise my spirits.

'Nevertheless, we have to think about what might happen should they detain you after all. You never know…'

'Well, they're unlikely to catch me red-handed. It *is* only a test. At most they can observe me walking around on the street. And I don't suppose that's a crime.'

'Right,' Wolfgang confirmed, stroking his chin. 'They'd have a solid reason for arrest only if they spied you stowing people away in the boot of the car. All they can do is prove that you've entered and left the GDR frequently.'

'Could it be,' I interrupted Wolfgang urgently as a thought flashed through my head, 'that someone has betrayed me?'

'You can never know, unfortunately.'

We continued weighing all the probabilities for a while. Finally, Fuchs said, 'We can ruminate over this endlessly – the fact is, it's your decision in the end. It's your freedom that's at stake.'

I nodded again and then asked Fuchs for a lengthy break. It must have sounded like a request for vacation. I could not go on.

After the real or imaginary confrontation with the 'leather jackets' I drove to my parents in Wuppertal, immediately went to bed in what used to be my childhood room, and did not want to leave it for days.

'What's the matter with you?' my worried mother asked.

'Nothing,' I droned.

'Are you lovesick?'

'No.'

'Is there something you can't tell your father?'

'No.'

'Then I'll call a doctor.'

'No,' I protested.

'Just accept my decision.' As caring as my mother was, she could be adamant in certain situations. Unsurprisingly, the doctor she summoned was unable to diagnose anything specific.

'There is no discernible explanation for your son's exhaustion,' he told my mother as he left.

'And it seems you won't give me a reason, either,' sighed my mother heavily as she left my room. Of course, I could have given her one, but I could not risk it. She would then have had to report everything to my father. My operations were not just little secrets tightly kept between mother and son. They were about far more.

I had always thought myself to be relatively adept at organising things. Actually, not a bad qualification for an escape helper. But the more action I saw, the more I understood that the importance of 'being able to organise' was limited in that context. Decisions often had to be based on intuition. Things could not be totally planned. Proceeding intuitively was perhaps not one of my greatest strengths. Besides, abstract danger wore down my nerves. I had imagined being arrested a myriad times, but now I was dealing with a lurking menace. I suspected persecutors or more of those 'leather jackets' everywhere.

***

From the outset, I had wholeheartedly committed myself to this project. But was I in the process of losing myself? Of utterly draining myself? Clenching my teeth as I lay in bed, I had to admit that my double life was causing me extreme stress. The lies, the excuses, the threadbare explanations for the days on which Barbara or my parents could not reach me. I had to be hellishly on guard not to contradict myself. And because I was hiding something, I no longer felt close to others. They felt the same way towards me. Disappointed by my secretiveness, which perhaps led to a certain distrust, they were drifting away from me. Not on purpose but rather in response to my peculiar behaviour. A great loneliness enveloped me. Unhappy and insecure, I buried myself deeper into my pillows.

Pure exhaustion shackled me to my bed. Over the next few days I mentally reviewed all the escapes I had participated in. They dominated all my thoughts. I could not easily process and digest all of the chaotic impressions and emotions. The stress I had tried to suppress during the operations remained stored in my brain and was now resurfacing. It usurped my dreams, which were often nightmares and visions of being arrested. But despite my fear of the leather jackets who may still have been lying in wait for me, despite my physical and psychological fatigue, I left my bed after a few days. It was useless to give in to brooding.

My will was unbroken. That surprised me after the days in Wuppertal. Despite the nightmares, I wanted to return to Berlin as quickly as possible. Solidarity was driving me. I had the same strong sense of making common cause with Wolfgang as I had towards my fraternity brothers. Someone on the outside could, of course, interpret our relationship in other terms – that he was putting me under pressure to continue following *his* agenda, which he professed was *our* agenda. Some of my friends later thought I had blindly followed Wolfgang. I see it differently. I was not a blind follower of either Fuchs or Schleyer.

Never in my life have I followed anyone blindly. In my eyes it was just such behaviour that had led to Germany's division in the first place. The vast majority of Germans kept silent under National Socialism, went along with Hitler's policies blindly and willingly, even though everyone saw the Jews being hunted on the streets, at least in the major cities. It was the total failure of common decency, a fact that still brings me to tears today.

I have followed no one blindly but rather have tried to judge people by what they did and how they spoke about it. And from that position, there was a feeling of standing shoulder to shoulder with Fuchs. Naturally, he had a vested interest in having me involved. That was obvious. But during the days in Wuppertal, I had sweated through so much that I was now convinced all was in order and that nothing could happen to me.

* * *

Things, however, were nowhere near in order anymore. What I did not know was that the Stasi had meanwhile infiltrated Wolfgang Fuchs's operation through Rainer Hildebrandt, the founder of the Checkpoint Charlie museum. A man whom Hildebrandt had innocently recommended to Fuchs turned out to be a mole. Part of the mole's mission was to investigate and betray me. I later found the relevant files, which contained a report on the last conversation that 'IM Manfred'[2] had

---

2 IM is the acronym for *inoffizieller Mitarbeiter*, the East German term for a private informant, an unofficial collaborator reporting to the East German State Security Service (Stasi).

with Wolfgang. The person had pressured Fuchs to help him smuggle his fiancée into the West as quickly as possible. She was purportedly a nurse in East Berlin and his great love. In the words of the East German files, this ruse was called a 'plan for the liquidation of a smuggling channel by means of arrest of all participants caught red-handed'.

From the files I also learned what had led to this promising plan: 'Given the fact that the courier, Heinz, basically enters the capital of the GDR only when smuggling takes place, he is to be placed under surveillance upon his next entry.'

Then in the same file I read Wolfgang's devastating comment, which struck me like a thunderbolt: 'Well then, I probably have to bring in my best man from Bonn.' Why for heaven's sake had he said that? Aside from the flattery that he considered me to be his 'best man', he had violated the simplest conspiratorial rule by mentioning Bonn. My greatest measure of safety lay precisely in the fact that I did not live in Berlin. To name the capital of the Federal Republic of Germany was sheer folly and immense carelessness. To me it meant that Wolfgang had not acted professionally. In the final analysis, he, too, was an amateur in this business. Otherwise, those words would never have crossed his lips. I am certain that Fuchs never intended to endanger me by anything he said and that he was simply unaware of how damaging his words were, but a little more caution wouldn't have gone amiss.

The test run was scheduled for mid-August. I travelled to East Berlin and picked up where I had left off the last time. My thoughts revolved around only one question: Was I being shadowed? Constantly looking behind me was too conspicuous. I was annoyed that I had not brought along a small mirror.

But would that have been any less obvious? A man who keeps looking in a mirror? Well, there were certainly very vain men who incessantly had to check the appearance of their hair. Maybe I would have managed that. But to me it seemed safest just to walk straight ahead and glance around occasionally while crossing the road. A completely normal gesture that would attract no attention.

Shop windows could also have been useful, but the GDR had no proper window displays. Even on Stalinallee (today's Karl Marx Allee), lined by the huge, elaborately decorated buildings for privileged comrades, there were few displays. The occasional shop did not invite people to press their noses against the window to stare at what was (or rather was not) on offer. The range of merchandise was simply too limited to show it off. Step by step, I approached Friedrichstrasse. Nothing struck me as unusual. Nor did I notice anything unsettling at the border. I felt greatly relieved.

'Everything went smoothly,' I reported to Wolfgang later. 'I suppose there was nothing to get so upset about after all.'

'You mean you were simply mistaken?' Fuchs enquired.

'I think so. The leather jackets didn't exist. I jumped to conclusions. If they were there, then I shook them off.'

'Are you sure?'

'Well, otherwise it would have gone differently today,' I said.

'You want to go back in, then?'

I nodded.

'That's good news.'

But the doubts deep down inside me had not disappeared. I would have liked to talk to someone about them, but I couldn't. Perhaps I could have asked Manfred or one of the other former tunnel builders for advice, but my relationship with them had never really become close. To get a fair assessment from them, I would have had to reveal too many details. Besides, I would have had to clear it with Fuchs. It would not have been good to go behind his back and then let him know I had changed my mind because of advice I had received from this or that person. Wolfgang himself was, of course, the wrong person to speak to. He, the eternal can-do man, would only have come up with persuasive counterarguments. My hesitation to confide in someone from the group also showed that I was more of a lone wolf, not someone who went with, nor needed, the pack. Looking back now, I am sure that if I had soberly thought through my experiences and doubts at the time, I would have come to a different conclusion. But that is not what I did then. I had agreed – and there was no turning back. 'The coast is clear!' That was the optimistic motto of our next operations. To this day, I still do not know whether I really had been shadowed.

We ran a few more successful escapes, including the 'double hit' of the two trips with the doctor's family that Schleyer had requested. By then it was already August. However, we were under Stasi surveillance during our last successful operation, as I later learned from the Stasi files. The Stasi wanted to be absolutely sure before arresting a diplomat. That made perfect sense – the whole story was an explosive issue. The GDR wanted international recognition, and detaining a diplomat usually tended to cause uproar. But precisely because the issue was so explosive, and because the Stasi wanted to be one hundred per cent certain, they let us get away with it before their very eyes – and I hadn't noticed anything at all.

TRAPPED

The doorbell rang. It was late, about 11 pm, 8 September 1966. Who could it be, I wondered, poring over my law books. I was not expecting my girlfriend. When I opened the door, a courier was standing before me.

'A telegram for you,' he said and handed it to me. I closed the door and read the message. It was from Fuchs and contained only two words: 'Call requested'. Then a Berlin telephone number. It was not his home number. 'Where was he?' I pondered.

'I'm supposed to call you,' I said when Wolfgang answered on the other end of the line.

All he said was, 'Can you come tomorrow? I need you in the evening.'

'But I can't fly until the afternoon.'

'That's OK. But I can't pick you up at Tempelhof airport.'

'Who will give me the information?'

'Furrer, he's reliable.'

That was true. Reinhard Furrer was reliable. The blond, bearded fellow, who later became an astronaut, was an important helper with Tunnel 57. We knew each other well. He had thought up an alias for his escape work. The name sounded like the protagonist in a spy thriller: Nikolayev. I liked Furrer a lot. We often sat together at Fatso's. I found him to be loyal, and a man of action. An engaging, impressive person. He had been there during the exchange of gunfire that had killed Sergeant Egon Schultz. Furrer had carried a weapon but told me that he had not used it. The gunman was an escape helper and friend, but the shot had not been fatal. As mentioned earlier, because the GDR denied access to the autopsy files until the re-unification of Germany, clarification of who had fired the lethal bullet had for many years been impossible. Later it emerged that the sergeant had been accidentally killed by his own people in the nocturnal crossfire.

Furrer was the first to have emerged from the tunnel on the eastern side and to tread no man's land. He was a bold man, both underground and in outer space. He died during an air show at the Johannisthal airfield in Berlin in 1995, killed instantly when the single-engine Messerschmitt he was flying crashed – twenty-nine years to the day after our meeting in Tempelhof.

'Hello, Volker,' Reinhard greeted me. It was about 4:30 pm. As we walked to his car, he said, 'Everything's pretty tight. We're driving straight to the Wall. On Zimmerstrasse is the City Café. I'll give you the persons' description there.'

'That's all right with me,' I replied. 'I hope they have decent coffee.'

'Certainly no watery, fake coffee,' Furrer laughed.

The café was almost full. In a far corner we found two free seats. The ambient noise level was perfect, and no one paid any attention to our conversation.

'Well?' I asked expectantly after the waitress had brought us two cups of coffee.

'I see you're raring to dive into another adventure.' Furrer gave me a roguish smile.

'It's more like I want to get it over with quickly. I'm a little tired at the moment.'

'Just watch out for yourself.'

'I will. Don't worry. So, who am I to meet today?'

'A man and a woman,' explained Furrer, taking a sip of coffee. 'A married couple, both about thirty. He'll be wearing a light grey summer suit; she's blond with a narrow face and pinned-up hair. She'll be wearing a white summer coat and carrying a white handbag. It shouldn't be a problem to recognise them.'

'OK. And what's the magic phrase?'

'*How far is it from here to Greifswalder Strasse?* The two of them then have to answer, *Three minutes from here.* Got it?'

'My brain is still working,' I said. 'And where is the meeting point? Everything went so fast yesterday.'

'Dimitroffstrasse, between Greifswalder and Prenzlauer Allee.'

'Then the code phrase really makes sense,' I said with a grin.

'It's what you call good planning. But we should leave now,' Furrer warned. 'Finish your coffee. It's on me.'

While he paid, I went outside and watched the sun slowly setting. Then we drove to Heinrich Heine Strasse.

The crossing there was a large checkpoint in an industrial zone near the Moritzplatz underground station. West German citizens were not the only ones who could enter East Berlin here. It was mostly used by postal vehicles and commercial trucks. In April 1962 Klaus Brüske and Heinz Schöneberger tried to ram through the barriers in a truck. The border guards opened fire, killing Brüske and seriously wounding Schöneberger.

'Good luck,' Furrer wished me after dropping me off. He drove away. Strangely enough, I gazed after him for a long time, until he turned at an intersection and was out of sight.

Around 5:30 pm I applied for a day visa for the umpteenth time. I had already successfully helped many dozens of people to escape. Not a bad track record over a period of about five months. The number would rise tonight.

After taking care of the border formalities, I walked over half a mile to the Jannowitzbrücke S-Bahn station, unfolding my 'Falk' street map of Berlin to find Dimitroffstrasse (called Danziger Strasse today) in Prenzlauer Berg, an area in the district of Pankow. Actually, I knew where it was, but I wanted to refresh my memory of the area. Although my many excursions to East Berlin had familiarised me with this part of the city fairly well, the folding Falk map was vital, especially when unexpected things suddenly occurred and I quickly had to look for another route back to where I had started.

The escape operation proceeded as smoothly as ever. Exactly according to plan. I used the S-Bahn from Jannowitzbrücke to Alexanderplatz. From there I took a taxi to the arranged meeting point, arriving at about 6:30 pm at Dimitroffstrasse, named after the Bulgarian resistance fighter and later prime minister, Georgi Michailovich Dimitroff. I quickly identified the woman in the white coat. She and her husband were walking up and down the street as though waiting for acquaintances with whom they wanted to spend the summer evening.

'Excuse me, how far is it from here to Greifswalder Strasse?' I asked when I approached them.

'Three minutes,' they answered together in a flash. Obviously, they had practised the response.

I quietly told them that we would take tram 74 in the direction of Müggelsee. Separately. 'And keep a distance of about twenty metres from each other until you get to the tram,' I whispered.

I repeatedly turned to look behind me on the way to the tram stop. Was anyone following us? But nothing aroused my suspicion. There was no leather jacket to be seen anywhere. The couple behaved normally, too. They did seem a bit tense, but compared to many others, they had their nerves well under control.

We changed to a bus, and at about 7 pm we got out at the stop in Wartenburg, a neighbourhood in the district of Lichtenberg. The place for the handover was a few minutes away by foot. I had given the location to Wolfgang just the day before, having already inspected this route and found it suitable.

Suddenly, I saw a car approaching us in the distance. I reacted immediately.

'Quick, into the cornfield,' I called to the escapees, and we rushed into the high, dense growth of cornstalks. An ideal hiding place.

'What do we do now?' asked the wife, her eyes dilated with fear as she looked at her white coat, which now had a few smudges.

'Wait and see,' I replied. 'We can't return to the road straight away. Maybe we're being watched.'

'But if the driver of the getaway car gives up and leaves?' The husband sounded very frightened.

'Don't worry,' I reassured them. 'He'll still be there. We won't stay here for longer than five minutes. I just want to be sure that everything is quiet again.' My heart was racing. The couple was right. Indeed, the Syrian must not linger too long at the appointed place. That would arouse attention in this remote and solitary area with little traffic.

After a few minutes I gave the all-clear. The vehicle I had considered suspicious had not come down our stretch of road again and had not suddenly parked. I had no idea that surveillance was focused only on the white Mercedes, which was to be inconspicuously 'accompanied' to the border.

'Get in quickly,' I instructed the couple when we had reached the car and I had raised the lid of the boot. 'And don't make a sound until the boot opens in West Berlin.' I stared into faces that expressed only one thing: 'We have risked everything. There's nothing more we can do now.' This moment was incredibly intense. I had to swallow hard. The courage of these people impressed me deeply. Would I have dared something like this if my freedom had been at stake? I think so, but one never knows.

I pushed down the lid of the boot. Hamdi Kamal started the engine. 'Can you give me a lift?' I asked the Syrian diplomat. 'I'm already running late.'

'Of course,' said Kamal. 'I'll let you out at the next S-Bahn or underground station.'

'That would be a great help. Thanks.'

We said nothing during the drive. Hamdi turned on the radio. The quiet classical music calmed us. Sitting in the passenger seat, I straightened up. The danger of no longer arriving at the border on time had been removed.

Hamdi dropped me off at an S-Bahn station, and I rode back to Jannowitzbrücke. Managed to get through that relatively unscathed, I thought, as I walked back along the Spree River, away from the bridge. As I entered the barrack at the checkpoint to exit East Berlin at Heinrich Heine Strasse, I did not notice a dark car parked right next to it.

Around 8:30 pm I pushed aside for the hundredth time the heavy felt curtain, which felt like a carpet to me. Suddenly, two men appeared out of nowhere to my right and left and grabbed my wrists. Within seconds, they handcuffed me.

'You are under arrest!' I heard a voice say. Then I was led outside and shoved onto the back seat of the car. The men who had arrested me took a seat on either side of me and instructed the driver to pull away. I offered no resistance of any sort.

Yes, it was a shock, but not a paralysing one. Feverishly I ran through in my mind what might happen next. I had always reckoned on this moment, but when it became reality, it all felt completely different. I could not believe that it had really happened. But it had happened, and I was not in the West and did not receive from Fuchs the happy news that all had gone smoothly. Nothing had gone smoothly, that much was clear as the car slowly drove through the night.

It was a fairly large Soviet-made vehicle, but not particularly comfortable. Sandwiched between the two men, I knew that fleeing was entirely out of the question. Even if I were to succeed in escaping from the car, where could I run?

'Where are you taking me?' I asked instead. I could not recognise much outside. No answer.

'What's going on? Where are we going?' Still no word. I saw that posing any more questions would be futile. I looked out of the window. After about a quarter of an hour, I was able to answer my own question: We stopped in front of the Stasi's investigative detention centre on Magdalenenstrasse (today a prison for women), a grey, featureless building. Ulrich Bahnsen had told me about this prison in Berlin-Lichtenberg. I was sure that Kamal Hamdi had also been arrested and that I would be interrogated straight away. After all, a diplomat was involved. What should I say? Deny, deny everything. Who could prove anything against me? Or would Hamdi betray me? I was led into an interior courtyard, but I could not see much. Gloom enveloped everything.

'Undress!' a uniformed man ordered as I was shoved into a pretty desolate room in the barrack. All I could make out was a table and a chair.

'Completely naked?' I asked.

'Yes.'

It was humiliating. I stood there stark naked after taking everything off, piece by piece, in front of the uniformed officers. In the next instant, every orifice was inspected. That was international practice, and the GDR was proud to meet the world standard.

After this unpleasant and fruitless procedure, I was allowed to put my clothes back on. The interrogations began immediately in a dismal, poorly lit room. The way to it passed through hallways no less grim. All the rooms smelled of sweat and Lysol.

'May I smoke?' I asked.

'No,' came the answer. 'And we ask the questions here. We know who you are and what you've been doing here.'

'I'm not doing anything at all here,' I countered.

'Then what do you need a city map for?' one of the interrogators asked. The folding map of East Berlin was the only piece of written material they had found on me.

'I don't know my way all that well in East Berlin. I only wanted to see the nightlife here. Students are curious.'

'You are not a normal student. You know that very well. You've been helping citizens of the GDR to flee.'

'No, I haven't. I'm here as a tourist.'

I denied everything, conceded nothing, which was not difficult. As long as they could not present any evidence of my crime, why should I admit it – even if they were right?

The first interrogation dragged on for hours. It was palpably clear that the people questioning me were under immense pressure. A diplomat had been arrested, so they needed results quickly in order to avoid straining foreign relations. But I did not deliver quick results.

Instead, I was asking myself the entire time what kind of mistake had led to my arrest. How had they known that escapees were hidden in the Mercedes? I just could not imagine how they had come to draw a connection between me and the Syrian diplomat.

What I did not learn until much later was that the GDR, even without using computers for the border checks, was already very advanced in a different area. Because Checkpoint Charlie was also used by diplomats, the border guards did not have complete control over the border crossing. The Stasi agents there thus used a special optical device with which they measured both the gap between the underside of a vehicle and the street and the angle of the rear wheels to the perpendicular. This instrument registered minute variations in load even if a vehicle like ours had a reinforced rear suspension. Any variations became apparent when the measurements of a vehicle upon its entry were compared to those upon its exit. All inbound and outbound cars – every single one of them – were noted along with the corresponding registration plates and measurements in long, neatly kept, handwritten lists, covering a period of three months. An enormous amount of time and effort.

The system worked. It enabled the Stasi to filter out several suspicious vehicles, making it easy to know which of them to focus on. In parallel, they compared the photographs of Kamal

Hamdi's Mercedes with the visa lists of West German citizens who had entered the GDR, me included. The result was convincing. It was a brilliant method.

In addition, there was my personal information obtained by the mole whom the Stasi had infiltrated through Rainer Hildebrandt. The mole knew from Fuchs that I was his 'best man from Bonn'. None of us had expected betrayal by the man who had claimed that he wants Fuchs to help his fiancée escape to the West.

After two or three hours the interrogators changed their tactics. They still did not have my confession. I did not know that they had compelling evidence. But now they revealed at least part of it. By then it was 5 am. The two uniformed officers stood up with a gesture of triumph. One of them, in his mid-forties, had a pasty face and long sideburns. He left the room and shortly after returned with another man in tow. It was Kamal Hamdi, the open door framing him like a picture. The Syrian said nothing. His face was ashen. After about a minute, he was led away. The look in his eyes told me that we were both in a hopeless situation. But I did not want to admit it either to the uniformed men or to myself.

'Well?' said the interrogator who had stayed in the room, his alert grey-blue eyes fixing on me cunningly.

'I don't know that man,' I said in a voice as resolute as possible and continued claiming to be a tourist. It seemed to me that lying was still the shrewdest strategy. But from then on I knew for certain that the diplomatic car had been searched and that the couple in the boot had been discovered. After my release I learned that Hamdi was said to have resisted arrest, though I did not find out any details.

After about half an hour, I was confronted with the young married couple, who also appeared in the door frame. They, too, were as pale as ghosts. Again, no word was exchanged. The strategy of the interrogators was clear. They were demonstrating that they had seized my people, that they did not believe at all that I was a harmless student.

The evidence was in fact overwhelming. From this moment on I realised it was absurd to pretend I was a tourist. I had assumed that the Stasi had no evidence and that I would not spend more than a night at Magdalenenstrasse. I had prepared myself for that, but now it was clear that I had underestimated the interrogators and what they knew. Around six o'clock in the morning, I had accepted the senselessness of further denial.

'Yes,' I finally admitted, 'I helped in the attempted escape.' The two interrogators looked at each other in triumph, but above all in relief. They were no less exhausted than I was.

After I had confessed, I was led into an ugly cell measuring three or four square metres. It was narrow and high; had an open, stinking bucket; a narrow wooden plank as a cot; and a tiny window opening beneath the ceiling. The interrogators did not seek anything more than an initial confession that night. The details could be spelled out later. I surmised that they had to write a short report for their boss, Erich Mielke, head of the Stasi, to provide the GDR government a basis for their next discussion with the Syrian government. Dead tired, I lay down on the cot, unable to think clearly anymore, and simply fell asleep. I was in the same position when a guard awoke me about three hours later. I must have slept like a rock.

After I had had a cup of watery coffee and two slices of bread with a hint of margarine, I was driven in a camouflaged, windowless van to Hohenschönhausen, the Stasi's investigative detention centre. It lay in the northeast of Berlin, the 'forbidden' part of the city. Forbidden because the entire complex was not permitted to be shown on any city map published by the GDR. (It was not marked on West Berlin city maps, either; only the road network was represented.) Hohenschönhausen was once a special Soviet camp but was taken over by the Ministry of State Security (MfS) and expanded with a new building in 1961. It housed the interrogation rooms and the prisoner cells.

I did not know at the time that we turned onto Genslerstrasse. The van was cramped, and I had no view to the outside. I focused on the sounds of the street, the drone of the engine, the humming of the wheels. A few minutes later it occurred to me that we were still driving straight ahead. I guessed – correctly, as I later found out – that we were on Landsberger Allee, which stretched nearly seven miles (almost eleven kilometres), one of Berlin's longest streets. The prison transport van stopped. A heavy sliding steel door closed automatically. I was allowed to climb out. I found myself in a kind of sluice, more precisely, in a room that resembled a spacious garage with a high ceiling. The walls and ceiling were white, and neon lights glared. There was a system to it. I had just emerged from a dark cubicle and abruptly walked into piercing light. It was a form of intimidation. After my eyes had adjusted somewhat to the harsh light, I was able to glimpse the sluice into which the van had driven. A couple of steps ascended into a long corridor lined by cells on both sides. A dirty yellow or green coloured paint covered the walls and ceilings. The only windows in the cells were glass blocks, which obscured everything beyond them.

So, I had landed in prison after all – for the simple reason that I had helped others escape from a much larger prison, the GDR.

CONFESSING WITHOUT BETRAYING

'Empty your pockets.' I was sitting in a bare room. The window overlooked a courtyard workshop. Out of my pockets came my ID card, my folding city map, a handkerchief, a necktie, two matchboxes, a ballpoint pen, a pair of sunglasses, and a brown leather wallet containing seven East German marks and twenty-five West German marks. Everything I had was recorded with Prussian precision.

The process of registering me followed. My height and weight were measured, my hair was defined as 'light blond ... parted on the left'. Eye colour: light brown. Special features: 'scars above both eyebrows'. They were the result of various childhood falls. Then I was fingerprinted and made to sit on a wooden swivel stool so that I could be photographed from the front and from both sides.

At the end I was handed the institutional clothing: a blue-and-white-striped shirt, a pair of saggy underpants, a pair of dark-blue trousers, and a similarly coloured jacket. Lastly, I was permitted to slip into a fetching pair of brown-and-yellow patterned felt slippers. I also received a toothbrush and toothpaste, a safety razor, and a fairly large plastic bowl. At first I did not know what this last item was intended for. Then I realised that it was absolutely essential. Shortly after wake-up at five am, a long hose ending in an iron pipe with an attached tap was noisily shoved through the iron door's small hatch was used for communication and delivering food. If the occupant did not rush to it with the bowl quickly enough, the warder, unmoved, just opened the tap, letting the water flow into the cell. The water was for drinking and washing, the sequence left up to the individual. There was no sink, though the cell did have a flush toilet with a seat but no lid.

Instead of a window, my cell had the customary window frames encasing glass blocks, which admitted only a hint of daylight. The upper half of the blocks was set level with the interior wall, the lower half level with the exterior wall. The resulting horizontal air vent could be closed with a horizontal wooden shutter. In all other respects the cell was more notable for what it did not have. No little closet for private use, not even a shelf. The only illumination was a weak lightbulb above the cell door, and it could be turned on only by an exterior switch or push button. At night it went on regularly at about five-minute intervals so that inmates could be monitored for any attempt to commit suicide. But what could they have used to attempt it in the first place? Even the safety razor could not be unscrewed to remove the blade.

The furniture included a narrow wooden table and two stools. The prison cots filled up most of the room. The wooden structures could hardly be called beds. Each was covered by a thin mattress, a sheet, and a blanket. No pillows. The head of each cot was slightly inclined. The occupant was not allowed to lie on the cot during the day.

I shared my cell with a GDR citizen of about my own age. He sat on one of the stools and looked at me with interest as the door closed behind me. Right away I thought he was surely there to help with the investigation – a spy with the mission of getting me to pour out my heart. Well, he can wait a long time for that, I told myself.

Richard's outstanding feature was the pallor of his skin. His hair was black but quite dull. He was rather shy and not especially talkative. He seemed a bit listless, for he no longer saw any prospects for his future. He had already lost his job, and after his release from prison he would find a society that would isolate him because of his incarceration. It was only later that I dubbed him Richard. We did not need names in the cell. There were no other inmates. He was simply *du*, the familiar form of address in German, just as I was only *du* to him.

Over time I got the impression that he was not a spy. He simply asked too few questions and did not want to know much. I never learned why he was being kept in Hohenschönhausen.

Upon hearing of my arrest, Manfred Baum immediately informed the lawyers Wolfgang Vogel (GDR) and Jürgen Stange (West Berlin). Requested by Fuchs to notify my parents as well as Schleyer, Manfred drove to Wuppertal with Joachim Schreiber to tell my parents personally about my arrest.

The two young men went to my father's office in Wuppertal-Elberfeld, where they introduced themselves as 'friends from Berlin'. My father, who certainly could be a bit gruff, inquired, 'Is there something I can do for you?'

'Thanks, but no.'

'And what brings you to my office?' he asked frostily.

'You don't have any idea what this might be about?' The question was rhetorical, of course. My father seemed irritated and now also a bit worried.

'I haven't got a clue, so let's stop beating about the bush.'

After some humming and hawing, Joachim finally pulled himself together: 'Volker is in investigative custody in East Berlin. We're very sorry.' My father was silent for a while, but his face betrayed his concern. Finally he said, 'Are you sure you mean my son?'

'Very sure, unfortunately,' replied Manfred.

And then they told him what they had been able to find out about me and my arrest. When they had finished, my father simply said, 'Well then, I suppose I'd better engage a lawyer for this pretty quickly.'

'Excuse me, Mr Heinz,' said Manfred politely but firmly, 'we've already informed the two lawyers who are best suited for this. Since it's such a delicate matter, we ask that this remain confidential.'

'Now look here! Just who, if I may ask, are these lawyers?' My father glowered, for he did not like it at all that the two young men sitting in front of him had taken things out of his hands. He, the director of a large company, had just been told what to do and what not to do.

'And by the way, we have informed Hanns Martin Schleyer about the arrest as well.'

'Why him, of all people?' My father's expression darkened still further.

'Volker informed him months ago.' My father's face was grim, and his voice choked when he finally said, 'All right then. There's nothing more for me to do, so you're free to go.'

Recounting this scene to me later, Manfred confessed, 'I think your father felt somewhat disempowered. His reaction surprised me somewhat.'

I could not suppress a smile.

'I can well imagine. But to be honest, I can also understand him to a point. He was both annoyed and worried and probably felt helpless.' I had known my father long enough to appreciate how difficult it was for him to understand my escapades. My arrest certainly didn't improve our already difficult relationship.

Dr Schleyer kept his word. Immediately after being informed of my arrest, he had travelled from Stuttgart to Bonn, to Werner Knieper, at that time the head of the Federal Chancellery. He, too, was a member of our Corps Suevia. Schleyer told him my story and asked him to help me. On 21 November 1966 he also wrote to Assistant Secretary Dankmar Seibt, the federal chancellor's personal advisor at the time. I have a copy of the letter:

Dear Mr Seibt,

By turning to you today with a request, despite the many demands on you, I can only hope that the nature of my concern excuses my appeal at this time. I am very concerned about the fate of one of my son's friends, who is a fellow fraternity brother and who was arrested and detained while helping people escape from the Zone in East Berlin. Over the past months I was in constant contact with the young man, Volker Heinz from Wuppertal, and was among the few who knew that he, acting purely out of idealistic motives and accepting the risk entailed, had been assisting many people... It would be of great importance if the Ministry for All-German Affairs and/or the Federal Chancellor's authorised representative in Berlin, Minister Lemmer, could take an interest in this case and urgently pursue whatever options there are, perhaps even as a priority. Perhaps you would be so kind, Mr Seibt, as to write a few supportive lines to those responsible in this matter, which is very close to my heart...

Respectfully yours,

H Sch

The letter did not miss its mark. The Office of the Federal Chancellor did indeed act, and the Ministry for All-German Affairs placed my name on the list containing the names of other prisoners to be exchanged. Schleyer had done for me precisely what I had hoped. He presumably saw himself not only as a fraternity brother but also in my debt for the role I had played in organising the escape of the Rittersberger family. But he would have intervened on my behalf even without that favour. Of that I am certain. I had always felt him to be a responsible man. His intervention made me a privileged prisoner. No GDR inmate could count on such backing. I surmise that Vogel therefore soon realised that I would be an excellent pawn in an East-West deal involving an exchange of captives serving long sentences. This accorded me a status that catapulted me into the same league as the spies. Although not an agent, I was nevertheless a 'special case'.

My father, who was not pleased that he could do nothing but wait and see what would happen, independently activated his own contacts in the political community, including Wuppertal's Otto Schmidt, a CDU representative in West Germany's lower house of parliament. However, Schmidt ended his efforts after the Office of the Federal Chancellor informed him of the proceedings already in motion.

***

'Come with me.' The next interrogation was about to start. I barely had time to get accustomed to my new 'home'. A so-called runner opened the cell door. His job was to fetch me for questioning and to return me to my cell. His power over us prisoners derived from his keyring, which he liked to rattle and shake and with which he practised artistic turning and locking movements, first in the air and then in the lock. Most of the jailers remained as obstinately silent as the prisoners. Likewise, I never tried to converse with them. Ulrich Bahnsen had told me how they responded to such attempts – not at all.

These security guards carried no weapons. They obviously did not fear being overpowered or injured by a prisoner. They could pull the alarm cord on the wall at any time. Everything in this Stasi jail was extremely simple and pragmatic. I have to admit that it was efficiently organised. Prussian love of order was clearly evident here. Every morning I was questioned for three to four hours, then again in the afternoon – just like a regular workday. At first, the interrogations sometimes took place at night as well. The hope was that sleep deprivation would elicit statements more readily, which, however, was a completely unnecessary exercise in my case.

It was always the same Stasi officer who questioned me. A lieutenant – at least that is how he introduced himself. He did not tell me his name. He had a carefully shaven face, light grey, watery eyes, and powerful bony hands that were in constant nervous motion. He seemed ambitious, like someone bent on making his career (which in part he achieved through me). He performed his work accurately and humourlessly. I never saw even a trace of a smile on his face. His grey uniform suited him perfectly.

There was also the 'major', a small man in his mid- to late forties with cunning eyes. He had been present during my first interrogation on Magdalenenstrasse. He once told me animatedly, 'I grew up in the GDR. I firmly believe in the superiority of socialism.' By then, the GDR had existed for 17 years, long enough for a young person to be shaped by it. Particularly in the early years, idealists believed in the new state. No wonder it attracted poets such as Bertolt Brecht. It was not until the Soviet Union intervened and introduced hard-line Stalinism that the liberals disappeared into prison or fled to the West.

The interrogation rooms were located in a special wing of the building. Apparently there were more than one hundred and twenty of them spread over several floors. They all looked the same: curtained windows with bars behind them, dreary wallpaper, a desk, a comfortable chair for the interrogator, an uncomfortable one for the prisoner being interrogated. A lamp stood on the light-coloured desk. One corner of the room had a grey steel cabinet in which all the documents relevant to my case were locked away after each interrogation session. The furnishings also consisted of a small cabinet with two sliding glass doors, through which I could see five or six books. The room was otherwise unadorned, the walls devoid of even a picture of Walter Ulbricht, the head of state. It was hard to imagine a bleaker place. It reeked of pungent cleaning agents even more than my cell did, and the stale air smelt vaguely of plastic.

The lieutenant showered me with photographs, hundreds of them. The Stasi considered me to be a serial offender. I was told it was well known that the husband and wife were not the only escapees I had helped. I was now to provide details on each of my operations, though they knew, of course, that virtually no one can remember *everything*, especially when the individual occurrences were similar.

The photographs served to jolt my memory. It was amazing all the people and actions they had captured on film, including Kamal Hamdi's diplomatic colleague, who had driven the Mercedes on the penultimate escape. That meant I had already been observed for quite a while. The pursuit by the men in the leather jackets had not been a figment of an overheated imagination; I had seen everything correctly. They had already had sufficient proof and could have seized me even then, but had let me go so as not to provoke diplomatic tensions. They couldn't be certain, but they thought it most likely that I would return. They were proven right. I have never learnt exactly when I came to their attention. But because of the measurements taken at Checkpoint Charlie and the information provided by the mole, they had probably had me on their radar for a long time before the men in the leather jackets had followed me.

'Do you know this person?' the smoothly shaven officer asked, pointing to one of the photographs he had spread in front of me. 'Is that the escapee whom you smuggled on that day?'

'Yes,' I said, 'but I don't know his name.'

That wasn't true, but I could admit recognising him because I knew that the former tunnel builder, like all the others in our group, would not be re-entering the GDR anymore and was therefore safe. Moreover, I wanted my acquiescence on this point to underscore my own credibility.

'And this person?'

'That is Manfred Baum.'

The rule in our group was to avoid betraying an accomplice, and I held to it. My friend Manfred had definitely ceased his participation, and at one of our many discussions at the pub he had told me that he would never again set foot on GDR soil. Things were clear with Ulrich Bahnsen, too. Neither he nor I had anything to fear. He was definitely 'out' and did not intend to become active as an escape helper ever again, or to enter the GDR. Stating that I knew him could not hurt him any more than it would Manfred.

I was repeatedly and stubbornly shown photographs of Heiko Neumann, who was occasionally engaged in my place.

'And this guy?'

'I don't know him.'

'Are you sure?'

'Very sure.'

Again and again, he showed me pictures of Heiko Neumann, but I insisted I had never seen him before. The lieutenant sighed more perceptibly from time to time, seemingly in disbelief. He was not wrong, but it was out of the question to betray Heiko. Just as I hoped he would not betray me if he were ever to be caught. What I didn't know was that he had been arrested not long after me.

* * *

My arrest must have come as a great shock to my family. From one day to the next, I had vanished. No one had an inkling of anything; everyone was now confronted with an accomplished fact. My sister, Marianne, recorded what it was like in our home when it emerged that I was in jail.

At first there was only silence and speechlessness, a weeping mother and a silent father. Everything had to be intuited. Father didn't speak much, no doubt also because he knew nothing and had no idea whom he could ask. There just wasn't any experience with this kind of thing – obviously not only for us. Just as little was said, much less judged, regarding the operation itself: Volker's actions, why, with whom, etc. If anything, there were only expressions of concern, above all about Volker's health.

For us as family members the problem was to get reliable information, including any through political channels – such as the Bonn ministries. On the other hand, we also had to 'keep our mouths shut'. It wasn't possible to get involved and help. We were unable to do anything.

As we gradually gained insight into the process, into the various steps of such procedures in terms of both arrest and efforts for release, when we heard the official names of persons or interlocutors, and when feedback became possible, everyday life relaxed but lacked key explanations and was marked by silent waiting.

Wait-and-see, forced inactivity. In October 1966 I was about to take my oral exams to graduate from secondary school, so I had plenty to occupy my mind with.

There was no relief until the first real contacts came into play and we received answers to questions we had posed. When we learned that Herr Schleyer could provide information on 'where in the prison and how long and when a possible trial would take place', there was hope, and peace of mind returned.

During my imprisonment, what I dreaded most was that my family would suffer greatly from their helplessness and the uncertainty of my fate. This description by my sister confirmed my fears. It hurts me every time I read it.

* * *

In the weeks and months that followed, everything the lieutenant had written down was gone over again and again so that the 'class enemy' – as the lieutenant branded the Federal Republic and, collectively, its citizens – would in his own ideologically charged words be unmasked and thereby be taken care of. Eventually, he came to speak of Fuchs.

'Was the terrorist Fuchs associated with imperialist secret services, specifically with American ones, as regards the smuggling operations?'

I couldn't believe that he had actually called Wolfgang a 'terrorist'. But broaching a discussion about it would have led nowhere. The lieutenant formulated my 'response' in finest bureaucratic German, the transcript of which I reviewed later:

> I became aware that, prior to an operation, the personal information of the GDR citizens who were to be smuggled was passed by Fuchs to a Bureau P 9 agent or middle-man unknown to me. The 'reliability' of the persons to be smuggled out is checked by that bureau in a manner unknown to me.

'P 9' (and 'X 10') were American secret service agencies, as I later learned. The prefabricated 'answer' was all the lieutenant's own work. It was put into my mouth. Why did I sign the document anyway? I was firmly convinced that the statements would not be taken as a confession in the West.

On another occasion the lieutenant wanted to know, 'How were you brought up by your parents?' The predetermined text, my alleged 'answer', lists five points:

> I believe I have identified the following child-rearing approach: 1. Politically and denominationally unaffiliated, but Christian in orientation; 2. Tolerance without sliding into weakness; 3. Recognition of the capitalist concept of property and its social structures; 4. The principle of one's own hard work as the precondition of a materially secure livelihood; 5. Caution when engaging with political groups.

Unsurprisingly, the lieutenant followed up with the question, 'What is your attitude towards the social conditions in the GDR?' I 'replied': 'From what I have heard in different conversations with people who have fled the GDR and with members of the West Berlin population, I think I may conclude that the social system in the GDR has a dictatorial character...'

This would not have pleased the lieutenant, but he betrayed no emotion. He just stoically noted my words, or rather his interpretation of my words. I signed everything without fighting over the wording. As I quickly found out during my first attempts to alter the wording, the lieutenant clearly regarded the wording as his domain, not mine.

Extensive transcripts were prepared for each session. They were rather ponderous and dry. 'I think I may conclude': that's not at all how I speak! I said this to myself each time I read through the many pages which I had to sign. Although my words had been 'adapted' into strongly ideological language, I read everything through closely to eliminate at least any crass factual inaccuracies and ensure that nothing had been completely made up. I never found anything genuinely wrong, however, and the ideological superstructure did not bother me. Clearly, the lieutenant was obliged to go through these motions.

I signed without batting an eyelid, page after page, escape after escape. This, too, was part of my strategy. I was prepared to cooperate as long as I did not endanger third persons. No one would believe that I didn't know anything at all. 'Controlled' cooperation, I concluded, could ultimately only have a positive effect on what still awaited me.

Most of the time, I sat on one of the two stools in my cell, thinking: Now you're paying for what you did. You're paying a price, one you can't pass on to others. You're paying with your own freedom because you helped others gain theirs.

Did I regret what I had done? No. I had helped people whose personal freedom had been highly restricted. Regret would have had to coincide with a guilty conscience, which I certainly did not have. Of course, in hindsight there were things I would have done differently. For instance, it had been very foolish to re-enter East Berlin after the encounter with the men in the leather jackets. But I have never been sorry about the basic decision to work as an escape helper. I had engaged in something that I accepted as absolutely right, and I wanted to do it as well as possible. I was aware at all times that it entailed great risks. Now I had to suffer the consequences and, most of all, learn to live with them. Already in those days, I was a rather rational person and tried to come to grips with my new situation as calmly and objectively as possible. Despite all my rational efforts, however, I only had partial control over my feelings. Fears of the future assailed me, especially at night.

One topic in particular preoccupied me: the commercial aspect of helping people escape. I always banished it from my thoughts and did not wish to know anything about financial entanglements in which my fellow helpers might be involved. Besides, I always calmed myself with the fact that I personally earned nothing from the operations and that money had never played a role in my involvement. But then I upbraided myself: Don't be so naïve. The more secure the border, the harder it is to overcome it, requiring even more time, effort, and money to bring people out. In addition, negotiating with family members or friends of sixty or seventy people, selecting and instructing the messengers, and much more – it was a full-time job. Wolfgang Fuchs never called it a day at 5.30. He never took a vacation. If he kept or had to keep part of the money, I did not find it morally reprehensible. I had somewhat less understanding for the consul. I knew he had been paid by Wolfgang, but never heard exactly how much. Nor did it interest me. As a federal government official, Dr. Rehlinger, later commented, I was 'by far the most serious case of a genuine, indisputably idealistic escape helper'. This appeared as a quotation in one of his letters in a federal government publication released in 2012.

* * *

It was by chance that I eventually found out the lieutenant's name. After four or five months of incarceration, I was sitting in the interrogation room, facing away from the wall and the wooden cabinet with the sliding glass doors. Up to that point I had never been able to read the titles of the books inside. I was not allowed to turn around. I always had to look directly at the lieutenant. Never once had I left my place when he left the room for a minute or two.

One day, though, I felt the temptation to do so. When the lieutenant made a brief exit again, I swivelled around on my stool, swiftly opened the cabinet containing a small reference library, and took out one of the books. Perhaps I could get a little closer to this man who never revealed anything personal about himself and could surprise him with this knowledge, show him that I was not to be underestimated. I glanced at the door. No footsteps. I hurriedly opened the book, and the very first page provided what I was looking for. A handwritten name: 'Bergmann'. I couldn't establish what kind of book it was because a second later I heard footsteps approaching. Hastily I returned the book to its place, closed the sliding glass door, and took up my prescribed position again on the chair. I feigned an air of innocence as the lieutenant resumed the interrogation. Back in my cell, I wondered whether this information could be useful to me. Is 'Bergmann' any kind of information at all? After all, knowing more than was permitted always meant a certain measure of power. Maybe it was the lieutenant's last name. If so, I had something on him. On the other hand, the fact that a handwritten name appeared in the book did not suggest that it was really the lieutenant's. I was grasping at every straw, no matter how thin.

A few days later, I was on the way back for more questioning, when I had an idea. Upon entering the room, I normally greeted the lieutenant with 'Good morning, lieutenant,' the prescribed etiquette in Hohenschönhausen. But on this morning I changed the ritual.

'Good morning, Mr Bergmann,' I said casually.

The effect of this greeting left not the slightest doubt as to the accuracy of my suspicion. Bergmann looked as though he wanted to sink through the floor. The names of people working for the Stasi were tightly kept secrets. But no other reaction followed the lieutenant's fleeting loss of composure. For seconds he said and asked nothing, but then he proceeded directly to the daily agenda.

'I'd like to know from you once again precisely how it was with this physician's family. The operation took place in the final phase of your activities.'

His short-lived silence was probably the most sensible reaction under the circumstances, but throughout that entire interrogation his chalk-white face never regained its normal colour. I wasn't sure what had so unsettled him. I only knew that I had played with fire. After all, *he* was obliged to keep his identity secret, not I. He had made a mistake, not I.

After my imprisonment, I read the Gauck Commission's personnel file on Mr Bergmann, a trained toolmaker from Saxony.[3] He rose to the rank of first lieutenant and sought further promotion. His hopes were disappointed, however, when his superiors attested to his 'reduced ability to work with increasing age'. He was 'transferred' to a less stressful position as 'Department Head in the Field of Human Trafficking Hostile to the State'. His personnel file also revealed that shortly after my release he received a medal and a reward in recognition of what the GDR saw as his successful work with me.

Years later, in November 2003, I wrote him a letter in which I asked to speak with him. 'I have no desire to criticise your work at that time. But I would like to write a book about my experiences and would therefore welcome it if you could agree to present things from your point of view.'

No reply ever came. I re-sent the letter by registered mail, receiving a countersigned return notice, but again received no answer. Thereafter I gave up trying to contact him, judging his silence as an indication that he did not wish to be reminded of our joint past. I could understand that. Bergmann had represented

---

3 The Gauck Commission was the government authority established by the West German parliament in August 1990 to preserve and reconstruct the records of the State Security Service of the former German Democratic Republic and to ensure public access to them. Joachim Gauck, a Protestant chaplain and one of the representatives of the anticommunist civil rights movement in East Germany, served from 1990 to 2000 as the inaugural head of the agency, the official title of which is the Federal Commissioner for the Records of the State Security Service of the former German Democratic Republic (Der Bundesbeauftragte für die Unterlagen des Staatssicherheitsdienstes der ehemaligen Deutschen Demokratischen Republik). More conveniently, it is usually referred to as the Federal Commissioner for the Stasi Records (Der Bundesbeauftragte für die Stasi-Unterlagen, or BStU).

views that history had consigned to the proverbial dustbin. Even if he had continued to believe in the GDR after the collapse of communism, his career path was considered a failure after the many revelations about the Stasi. It must have been difficult for such a person not to feel as though he were in the dock. Moreover, accommodating me would probably have required a personal interest in my fate.

Bergmann never struck or castigated me, although at that time, the 1960s, interrogations were conducted quite robustly. I have nothing to reproach him for and bear him no ill will. In my eyes he was a cogwheel in the Stasi machinery. The aim was either to lead people back to a virtuous socialist path or to wear them down. The GDR did that with psychological terror, which it mastered to perfection. The reason it did not succeed with me was that I felt no guilt and that I quickly accepted my incarceration. In addition, I was healthy and always forward-looking. Nevertheless, none of this completely protected me from plunging into the innermost depths of my soul.

Looking north along Friedrichstrasse from West Berlin into the East in summer 1960. The cyclist is about to cross Zimmerstrasse, along which ran the white line marking the border after Checkpoint Charlie came into being. Later events would render the site far more dramatic. (Courtesy of Allan Hailstone)

By October 1961, this was the scene at the same spot as Soviet tanks faced off against their US counterparts. By the mid-1960s, this tension had led to an almost total segregation. (Courtesy of the USAMHI)

A late 50s shot of Friedrichstrasse station, which served both the S-Bahn and U-Bahn. At the time of this shot, anyone could travel by rail or on foot between the two sectors of Berlin while undergoing few, if any, formalities. Things were to change drastically. (Courtesy of Allan Hailstone)

Potsdamer Platz, 1962. The sign is a DDR sign facing East and denotes the number of metres to the actual border, or to the 'end of the democratic sector', but it is marooned on the Western side of the Wall; it must itself obviously lie in East Berlin. (Courtesy of Allan Hailstone)

On Friedrichstrasse, the American authorities question the driver of a BMW bubble car with a West Berlin licence plate (B-) that has just come from East Berlin. (Courtesy of Allan Hailstone)

Bernauer Strasse, 1962. This notice, headed MURDER, asks 'Who knows the shooter?' and offers a 3,000 Deutsche Mark reward (then about £300) for the capture of the border guard who shot a refugee swimming across the River Spree (i.e. on West Berlin territory) while attempting to escape from East Berlin. (Courtesy of Allan Hailstone)

This bleak landscape shows the view northwards from the West Berlin end of Wilhelmstrasse at its junction with Kochstrasse. Wilhelmstrasse continues northwards until it reaches Unter den Linden, near Brandenburger Tor. (Courtesy of Allan Hailstone)

WIR FORDERN: FRIEDENSVERTRAG MIT BEIDEN DEUTSCHEN STAATEN U. ENTMILITARISIERTE FREIE STADT WESTBERLIN

Political slogans across buildings and on public transport were commonplace in East Berlin, usually in yellow on red backgrounds. This slogan states: 'We demand a peace treaty with both German states and a demilitarised free city of West Berlin.' (Courtesy of Allan Hailstone)

The author as a student in 1963. (Author's collection)

The smuggling car and its trunk. (Author's collection)

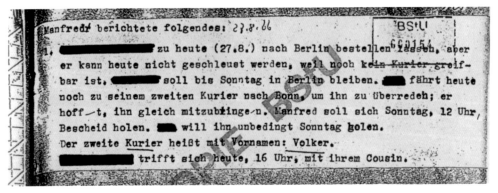

An excerpt from a report by Stasi spy IM 'Manfred', who was introduced to Wolfgang Fuchs. (Author's collection)

Above: The author in 2016 at Hohenschönhausen, the Stasi's main prison complex, where he was imprisoned. (Courtesy of Peter Vorlicek)

Right: A 2016 photograph of a watch tower on the perimeter of Hohenschönhausen. (Courtesy of Peter Vorlicek)

A corridor in the cellar at Hohenschönhausen (called the U-Boot or submarine) where prisoners were tortured. (Courtesy of Peter Vorlicek)

One of the cells at Hohenschönhausen at a later date. Water basins did not exist in the Hohenschönhausen remand prison in the 1960s. (Courtesy of Peter Vorlicek)

IN THE TWO-MAN CELL

In moments of darkness it was sometimes good to think about all the people I had helped in the past year and who could now start afresh in freedom. But this did not always console me. The isolation in our two-man cell was oppressive, and my mental state worsened week by week. After three weeks I was deeply depressed. I was in investigative custody. Eventually, I would be brought before a court and sentenced. And then? Despite my measured cooperation, I was left in uncertainty. The punishment could be severe, of that I was aware. Ulrich had received five years. I had to reckon with twice that much time.

Lack of sleep was getting the better of me. At night the light was turned on and off at short regular intervals, waking me each time. At first, I tried to cover my face with the blanket, but that was forbidden, as I was menacingly instructed. Only when I got used to lying on my back and sleeping with my forearm over my eyes did things slowly improve. More than twenty years after my release, I still assumed this position to fall asleep. It was one of the wounds inflicted by my incarceration, a deeply rooted reflex.

I had my problems with the wooden plank bed, too. It was much too short. Because its head section was inclined 25°, I had to inch my way towards the foot of it. But that meant that my legs dangled over the end. I was barely able to sleep.

The monotony and futility of such an existence, the lack of orientation, and the absence of a view to the outside world all began to wear me down. There was no music, and initially no books, either. There was nothing to make life more tolerable. The food, too, was extremely meagre. In the morning there was a slice of bread without butter or even margarine. The hard, dark bread was spread only with an artificial jam. Lunch usually consisted of vegetable stew made of lentils or beans, into which a few pieces of meat were added on weekends for variety. In the evenings we received slices of bread and sausage. At breakfast, we would be given watery, fake coffee, purportedly laced with 'Hängolin', a substance said to inhibit the libido of inmates in order to avoid sexual assaults. As absurd as it sounds, all this made the interrogations seem almost like welcome diversions.

At night in particular I was assailed by thoughts of the worries that I was causing my mother and father, my brother and sisters, my girlfriend, and all my friends. Had I been inconsiderate? Would they understand what I had done? Would my absence change the relationships I had? Bathed in sweat and often plagued by nightmares, I would eventually fall asleep, exhausted.

Depression is a destructive phenomenon. Anyone suffering from it feels utter hopelessness without being able to resist it. To me it seemed that nothing I said or did mattered at all. That was what the interrogators intended. It was a situation in which the inmates made confessions, often false ones, just to find some peace. It is no longer important what you do or don't do, for life is no longer important. Fortunately, I was never overcome by thoughts of suicide. Never once did I consider giving up altogether.

My 'roommate', Richard, suppressed his loneliness by communicating with our cell neighbour. They used a primitive system of knocking: one knock for A, two knocks for B, three knocks for C, and so forth. A single word could take minutes to spell out; a relatively long sentence, hours. I did not want to join in. It was too tiresome and seemed childish to me. Anyone in the neighbouring cells – and doubtless the jailers as well – could listen in, so it was utterly impossible to exchange secret messages in this way. If these 'conversations' had at least been about ingenious attempts to escape, I would presumably have been the first to participate.

'This knocking is bound to backfire,' I told Richard, 'if it achieves anything at all. We've landed in Absurdistan here.'

'So what?' he said. 'At least it makes me feel less alone. I learn where the others come from, what they're accused of. Sometimes there's also an address that can be useful after one gets out.'

I could see what he meant. But in my state of leaden indifference, I rejected everything. One evening, when I noticed that a self-destructive spiral of thoughts was literally strangling me, I realised that I had to break out of this. Enough, I admonished myself. You have to fight, or you'll leave prison a broken man. Use your reason. It has always helped you. In the fraternity you learned that survival takes discipline. You could get drunk in the evening, but you had to get up again at seven the next morning and go to your fencing lesson. You'd better pull yourself together and get over your lameness. Vegetating won't improve anything. Come up with something that will put you back on track!

My inner self was right, of course, and I tried to obey. I began with push-ups, a hundred of them every day in the fully enclosed roofless cage into which we were released to get some fresh air. Our indoor cell was much too cramped and stuffy for such an activity. These open-air cages, some 15 of them in a row, were surrounded by walls approximately 5 metres high. Wire mesh covered the open area on top of the walls where guards armed with machine guns constantly patrolled. In addition to the push-ups, I also began running in small circles to the extent possible, given the dreadful floppy prison slippers. I wanted to fight my mental instability with physical strength. I soon felt fitter and less at the mercy of the system. I had begun actively resisting the effects of captivity. They would not let me starve, nor would they beat me, but they still had enough other methods for achieving their goals.

I pushed myself to analyse my situation. What was a realistic prospect for the future? Suppose I were to receive a ten-year sentence. How many weeks would that make? 520. Good grief! No, don't even think about it. I couldn't fathom that amount of time at all, especially in relation to the few weeks I had survived so far. OK, next thought. Did the GDR grant early release for good conduct? I wasn't sure but assumed that I could probably expect to serve sixty to seventy per cent of my sentence. That meant I should reckon with six years, seven at worst. In other words, the time scale was clear. I was twenty-three years old and would be thirty in seven years. 'Volker,' I asked myself, 'do you know any thirty-year-old law students?' Two names occurred to me right away. 'There you are, then everything is OK after all. Life doesn't end at thirty. You can still always finish your degree. It's not half as bad as you think.'

After this calculation, I felt distinctly better. I sensed that I had been able to turn my struggle against depression in a promising direction. I only had to cope somehow with these seven years and, above all, accept them as part of my life. I had a future, albeit not an immediate one, but it *was* within reach. This realisation helped my determination grow again. I wondered how I could make the most sensible use of my prison term. As in every other civilised country, there must be training opportunities in GDR prisons, too. Maybe I could become a cook or a cabinet-maker, although I had to ask myself whether the food we received was really prepared by a trained cook. I imagined other options as occupations, too – electrician, plumber, something manual in any case. They certainly would not admit me to Humboldt University, and I could only dream of taking correspondence courses.

Dreams, particularly daydreams, were ideal for escaping prison life for a while. I tried to distract myself by thinking back to opera performances, concerts, films, or poems. In the evenings I would go to the theatre or to a concert. (I remembered especially well the famous violin concerto by Felix Mendelssohn Bartholdy in the Berlin Philharmonic Hall.) I attended a poetry reading and went to the opera. I vividly recalled an evening with my mother, who had taken me during my final year in secondary school to a performance of Friedrich von Flotow's romantic opera *Martha*. I found the opera rather dreary, especially the plot. Lady Harriet, the protagonist, seemed bored as well and teamed up with her servant and confidante, Nancy, to hatch a plan to escape the dreariness of her daily life. It now struck me as topical, relevant. Maybe that is why the performance kept swirling around in my head.

'I found the whole thing quite naïve, almost kitschy,' I told my mother on the way home. 'Women are just somewhat more playful and emotional than men,' my mother replied with a smile. She was the classic post-war mother who had no career ambitions of her own and whose children were the most important thing of all. Although she was easily moved to tears, she had a rather sharp tongue, a weapon with which she often defended us.

These excursions through my memories were beautiful but, unfortunately, I was not a renowned conductor who knew twenty scores by heart. Occasionally, I tried dealing with my situation by reciting set works I had learnt at school, such as Friedrich Schiller's *Song of the Bell* or the opening of Homer's *Iliad*.

* * *

While I was reciting to myself and attending imaginary theatre performances in my cell, the first steps on my behalf were being taken in the western part of the Federal Republic. I had no inkling of it, of course. On 29 October 1966 my father wrote to Hanns Martin Schleyer:

Dear Dr Schleyer,
Last Wednesday at the Bonn-Wahner airport, I met with Assistant Secretary [Ministerialrat] Dr. Rehlinger, who is the right-hand man to Permanent Under-Secretary of State [Staatssekretär] Krautwig in Berlin. Yesterday I duly received a call from that same gentleman and was instructed to send my son a package that will be delivered through the Stange/Vogel connection. It was also indicated to me that the matter is in the best of hands and that it is seen very positively. I informed him of your efforts, which he welcomed, and he awaits your letter via Bonn.

In response to my explicit question as to whether I should engage additional persons, he said there was no need.

I share this with you for your information and express my sincere thanks and also those of my wife for the great lengths to which you have gone thus far with respect to this matter.

With kind regards,

Georg Heinz

Four days later, 2 November 1966, Jürgen Stange, the lawyer, wrote to my father:

Dear Mr Heinz,

Your letter of 29 October arrived yesterday... The status of things remains unchanged as of yet. The investigations are in progress and will not be completed for six to eight weeks. The arrest warrant was based on section 21, subsec. 1 (Organised Inducement to Flee the Republic) of the StEG [Strafrechtsergänzungsgesetz, Criminal Law Supplementation Act].

Correspondence is permitted once a month. I therefore ask that a letter be sent to me in November. I will forward it. In addition, DM 30 per month can be transferred at a 1:1 exchange rate. I will gladly mediate this matter as well. So as not to lose time, I have already advanced DM 60. Your son can start by buying food or cigarettes with this money.

As soon as the package arrives, I will forward it.

Sincerely,

J. Stange

Attorney-at-Law

All the while, I kept looking for ways to distract myself in Hohenschönhausen. One day, as I looked over at Richard, I suddenly had an idea.

'Didn't you have Russian in school?' I asked my taciturn cellmate. We still had not spoken much with each other. Richard was distraught in prison, saying to me once that he was without hope and that nothing mattered. However, I had nevertheless learnt that he came from Dresden and that even as a schoolboy had not been able to adapt to the system in which he lived. It surprised me because I found absolutely nothing rebellious about him.

'Of course, every kid has to learn Russian here,' my cellmate replied.

'Do you think you could teach it to me?'

Richard was taken aback.

'Hardly. I've forgotten most of it. And we have neither a grammar book nor a dictionary. I don't think I'd be much help to you. I'm not a teacher.'

I did not relent, refusing to give way to Richard or the jailers.

'Can I at least have a little writing material?' I asked one of the warders. 'Paper and pencil? And a German-Russian dictionary?'

'Nothing doing,' came the cursory answer. 'That's not meant for you.'

'As of when could it be meant for me?'

'I don't decide that,' retorted the jailer.

(I waited four months to receive paper, pencils, and a dictionary. I'm not sure, but this 'concession' may already have had something to do with the negotiations that were underway.) I triumphantly sat down next to Richard.

'It will work, after all,' I said encouragingly.

'And now how do you want to go about it?' He looked at me as though I were not in my right mind.

'Say a word in Russian.'

'Chelavyek.'

'I can remember that easily. It sounds like "cello", then "vek."' (In German 'weg' translates as 'gone'.)

'Well, you can learn a language that way, too, of course,' Richard sneered. I didn't react.

'And now please draw me the individual letters in the air so I can imagine them. I once learned ancient Greek at school, and that alphabet is said to be quite similar to the Russian one.'

'Am I supposed to admire you now?' Richard continued, looking me up and down.

'Of course. And to raise your level of education a notch higher, I can tell you that the word *Cyrillic* comes from the Bulgarian monk Cyril, who brought the Greek alphabet to Russia along with the Christian faith.'

'I'm impressed,' came the deadpan response.

'You should be. But let's get started now.'

Richard could not escape my tenacity, indeed he had no other choice in our cramped cell. From then on, he taught me the basics of Russian and even developed a certain ambition when he saw that I was following him and could remember what I had learnt. I think this mental activity did us both good.

After a solid six weeks in Hohenschönhausen, I was at least allowed to smoke again. I could pay for the cigarettes with the money transferred through Jürgen Stange. I was told only that a small sum of money was available to me. Naturally, I did not yet know why. I was also permitted to write my parents a neutral letter. The conditions of my confinement were not to be mentioned, however, or the letter would be confiscated immediately. So I wrote only, 'I am well, and I hope you are, too.' Thereafter I received two or three small packages from them, which Richard and later cellmates regarded with silent envy, although I shared the contents.

It was months until I met with a lawyer, but I guessed that someone was working on my behalf in the background, as had been the case with Ulrich. They had a prisoner's account set up for me to receive money transfers. I could use coupons to order cigarettes, which were brought to me in the cell. I didn't know the details of the bookkeeping, and I didn't care. The main thing was that I had tobacco and matches again. Richard used the spent matches to draw the Russian letters on our cell's wooden table, enabling me to learn one word after another. After my incarceration, whenever I could lay my hands on a Russian newspaper, I was able to read it at least well enough to get the gist of it. Richard also taught me Russian folksongs that he had learnt at school, including 'I Love You, Life'. The life-affirming words were both so poignant and consoling and the contrast to our 'life' so great that this song sometimes brought tears to our eyes. But learning Russian vocabulary did not even begin to fill the many free hours.

'We have to occupy ourselves with something else. Look at you; look at me. We have to do something, or we'll go crazy in here. Can you play chess?'

My cellmate nodded but gave me another irritated look.

'We need a chess board.'

'You're funny,' quipped Richard.

'The table!' I exclaimed.

'Yeah, the table is a table,' Richard countered.

'It's a board!'

'OK, it's a board.'

'All we need to do is to somehow come up with black and white squares. I already have an idea.'

'You and your ideas.' Richard shook his head.

'They're occasionally better than you think,' I explained self-confidently. 'With the burnt matches, we'll draw lines on the table. The squares don't have to be completely black. Just a hint of colour will do, don't you think?' Richard was visibly impressed, but then frowned: 'Yes, but we have no chess pieces, and we can't very well carve any.'

'Hmmm,' I mused, looking around the cell. My gaze drifted to our mattresses. They were held together by cords and perforated buttons. Hoping the cords would be sufficient to keep the mattresses from falling apart, we removed the buttons by simply endlessly twisting them. Fortunately, each mattress yielded a set of sixteen figures, with a few spare figures to boot.

'You have wantonly destroyed prison property,' observed Richard with mock disapproval.

I grinned. With the used matches, we labelled the black figures with appropriate letters: K for king, Q for queen, R for rook, and so forth. We coloured the white pieces by applying some of our chalky toothpaste to the buttons and then relabelled them with the matches. To be honest, the chess games we played were not gripping, but that didn't matter. The main thing was that they distracted us from whatever devastating thoughts would otherwise have haunted us.

After our chess figures had been confiscated twice, our hobby ended. On both occasions the jailers took them on Saturdays when Richard and I were herded into the shower room. That killed the chess game. After many weeks the books that I was finally allowed to read were a small consolation. They were not always of much benefit, particularly since many of them fell into a literary category I thought of as 'combat books'. They were often about the development of socialism or the glorious collectivisation of agriculture on *kolkhozes* - collective Soviet farms - and 'agricultural production cooperatives' (LPGs). Readers were to be persuaded that everything in the GDR was, naturally, much better than in the West. Having no alternatives, I nevertheless greedily devoured every line.

But there were also pearls among the randomly selected set of four books that the 'librarian' – usually a soldier, and strangely always one with a strong Saxon accent – drew from a wooden pushcart and dismissively threw onto the cell door's service hatch, from which the books sometimes fell to the floor. I once could not believe my eyes when I found myself holding Max Frisch's *Mein Name sei Gantenbein* (1964; *A Wilderness of Mirrors*).[4] Were people in the GDR really allowed to read Max Frisch? I didn't know. To me, the novel was primarily about changing identities. Well, that certainly fits me, I thought.

---

4 English translation by Michael Bullock (London: Methuen, 1965).

BACKROOM DEALS

'You're going somewhere else today,' growled the guard on duty as he brought me out of the cell one morning in early November. As usual, we walked through the poorly lit corridor towards the interrogation wing.

'Where are we going?' I asked, surprised that he was talking to me at all.

'You'll see.'

The room into which I was led was larger than Lieutenant Bergmann's and was furnished with a more opulent desk. Transparent white nylon curtains gleamed before the barred windows, which were framed by colourful drapes. Bergmann's office was not as 'cosy'. On top of a small cupboard there was even a television set.

'Do you want to watch the news with me?' asked the Major with feigned nonchalance.

What on earth is going on, I thought feverishly. The Major would hardly have 'invited' me without a hidden agenda. This was certainly a trick, but what could it be? For lack of a better idea, I simply said, 'Sure.'

The Major smiled slyly. He was considerably better looking than Bergmann. He turned on the TV. We were joined by the lieutenant, and the GDR news broadcast, *Aktuelle Kamera*, started on the hour. It was a rerun of the previous night's transmission on 27 November 1966. A pale newscaster announced something that at first I did not understand. Then I pricked up my ears. He reported a change in the government of the Federal Republic on 11 November. The Free Democratic Party, the FDP, had withdrawn its four ministers from Chancellor Ludwig Erhard's administration, triggering a government crisis. The larger coalition partner – the CDU and its Bavarian sister party, the Christian Social Union (CSU) – had nominated a new candidate to run for the office of chancellor. Kurt Georg Kiesinger, the former prime minister of Baden Württemberg, had won on the third ballot. He had become the third chancellor of the FRG, elected by the CDU/CSU and the former opposition and now co-governing party, the SPD. Thus the two largest parties in the lower house, the Bundestag, had formed a new governing coalition.

This first so-called Grand Coalition at the federal level consisted of an idiosyncratic blend of politicians who for many years had fought each other tooth and nail and now had to work together. Franz Josef Strauss (CSU) became the finance minister, Karl Schiller (SPD) the minister for economic affairs, Herbert Wehner (SPD) the minister for All-German Affairs, and Willy Brandt (SPD) became vice chancellor and foreign secretary. I knew immediately that this was an enormously significant event. This would not only change the Federal Republic, but would also have an impact on its relationship with the GDR. The political situation was bound to change in many ways. I presumed it was not without good reason that the Major and Lieutenant Bergmann let me watch this broadcast. They themselves said nothing, but I instinctively felt what they were thinking: that SPD policy could facilitate a certain degree of rapprochement between the two Germanys, perhaps even the abandonment of the Hallstein Doctrine. The Major turned off the television and all of a sudden said, 'We once hung posters with the words "Friede für die ganze Welt" [Peace to all the world]...'

'No,' Bergmann interrupted, 'It read, "Frieden für die ganze Welt."'

The Major resumed, 'You see, quibbling over the right formulation almost makes us forget how central the peace policy is for our government, in contrast to the revanchists in the West. Did you know that Kiesinger was a Nazi?'

I knew it, but I also knew about the expansionist nature of communist ideology.

I was surprised that Bergmann had interrupted the Major – until it occurred to me that this conversation, too, had probably been rehearsed. The two uniformed men wanted to convey to me something of their deep communist and humanitarian persuasion. They played their parts damn well, for I did in fact ask myself whether they wanted to compromise me, to show me how little peace meant to me. Or were they hoping to win me over to their socialist idea of peace? Did they want me to change sides?

They gave no further explanation for why I had been invited to watch television with them. 'Enough for today,' said the Major, breaking the silence. 'The lieutenant will continue with you.' Bergmann stepped towards the door and called for the jailer. I couldn't really make head or tail of the whole episode.

* * *

Efforts in West Germany to have me released had meanwhile moved into high gear. In the exchange of prisoners or the purchase of their freedom, the key player on behalf of Bonn's Ministry for All-German Affairs was the West Berlin lawyer Jürgen Stange who had his office on Schlüterstrasse. He was authorised to conduct negotiations, but not to conclude them. Stange's opposite number was the East Berlin lawyer Wolfgang Vogel, who acted formally on behalf of the prosecutor-general of the GDR, a Stasi member himself.

Vogel, too, was authorised to negotiate on his own, but could not take final decisions. However, he had access to Erich Honecker, who at that time was still the secretary of the Security Commission of the Central Committee of the GDR's ruling party, the so-called Socialist Unity Party (SED). Honecker was not appointed to the party's position of General Secretary until the early 1970s. Vogel had to clear his actions with the Ministry of State Security. Of course, Walter Ulbricht, head of state and Mielke's superior, was involved in important cases as well.

Without the top level duo of Vogel and Stange, no substantial progress was possible. Vogel was responsible for negotiating the wish list the SED had compiled of persons to be released. I assume that the Federal Republic still possesses these lists but has not published them for reasons of data protection. It goes without saying that the West German government had its lists, too. The mutual task was to harmonise both lists somehow: a search for political equivalence. Some of the names were checked off without a problem, but the two sides did not always get what they wanted. I suppose that certain cases only progressed gradually and were deferred, if necessary, until a more favourable opportunity emerged. Bitter battles were fought. One can imagine what freedom or continued detention could have meant for the people involved. But did they even know about these negotiations?

Heinz Felfe's case, for example, triggered major contention. Born in Dresden, Felfe had been trained in foreign espionage by the SS at the Reich Security Head Office in Berlin. After the Second World War he worked for the West German Federal Intelligence Service, eventually becoming the head of its KGB section. After living for years as a double agent, he was revealed to be a KGB spy and arrested on 9 November 1961. By that time he had severely harmed many people by exposing CIA agents in both the GDR and the USSR. Felfe was sentenced to fourteen years in prison. The GDR wanted to buy his freedom straight after his sentencing, but the West German government refused. Not until the GDR threatened to shelve the entire West German policy of buying people's freedom was Felfe eventually released. Soon thereafter he was appointed associate professor of criminology at Humboldt University in East Berlin.

Felfe played a role in my case as well. Vogel had calculated that, like the top spy, I would be sentenced to fourteen years in prison. Through Stange he proposed to the Bonn government that I be traded for Felfe. The West German side was outraged by this proposal, as though Vogel had taken leave of his senses. They asserted that Felfe had sent vast numbers of people to their doom, that his case and mine could not be compared, and that such an exchange would be totally unbalanced. They argued that I, Heinz, was an idealist; Felfe, a hard-line, unscrupulous double agent. The one had acted selflessly; the other had clearly operated to his own advantage. No, the proposed deal was out of the question.

Stange was a master of his trade. In 1963 he had organised and helped carry out the very first buying out of prisoners. He had taken the agreed-upon sum with him on the S-Bahn from Lehrter Strasse to Friedrichstrasse, where Stasi Colonel Heinz Volpert – Vogel's supervising officer – received the money. In return, Stange received the prisoner, with whom he returned to West Berlin on the S-Bahn. No cash payments took place after this case; credit notes were issued instead. The GDR used these credit notes to buy goods it urgently needed, items ranging from rare metals and computers to specified sums of money and loans. The products were ordered and delivered until the credit notes were depleted or renewed. Colonel Volpert played a pivotal role in such transactions. Through Alexander Schalck-Golodkowski, a high ranking officer in the East German economics ministry and a Stasi officer, he operated an extensive network of firms in the FRG established for the sole purpose of acquiring hard currency. The German Protestant Church was also involved in the business of procuring coveted commodities, as it provided for the smooth transfer of money from secret funds of West Germany's federal budget. To me, this connection between prisoner exchange and commodity trade shows that the principal human trafficker was the GDR, not the idealistic escape helpers.

Whereas letters between Stange and Vogel and the Bonn government are archived, and much of the correspondence has been published, letters between Vogel and the GDR government have not yet surfaced. Vogel's main correspondents were presumably Mielke, Prosecutor-General of the GDR Josef Streit, Volpert, and, later, Honecker. Volpert was the pivotal figure in the exchange of prisoners. He reported directly to Stasi chief Mielke and is said to have helped decide who was permitted to be bought out, and for what price. Volpert was a trained agriculturalist. Together with Schalck-Golodkowski, Volpert wrote a doctoral thesis on these transactions and submitted it to the School of Law in Golm near Potsdam. The title was *Avoiding Economic Risks and Generating Additional Foreign Currency*. He died under mysterious circumstances in 1986. His body was found in the sauna of his Berlin home.

Apart from Volpert, Vogel had two more important interlocutors. One was the then Prosecutor-General of the GDR Josef Streit, who had begun his working life as a book printer and had then gone on to an 'exemplary career in the *Workers' and Farmers' State*', as a *Spiegel* obituary put it in July 1987. It further stated that Streit, a trained 'judge of the people', made crucial contributions to the GDR's legal system – which he regarded as the model opposing the 'Class-based Justice of the Weimar Republic' (the title of his doctoral thesis). Streit presided over all public prosecutors of the GDR and was a real hard-liner.

The third man with whom Vogel had regular contact was Mielke himself. No doubt there were also occasional encounters with Honecker, but few details are known. Vogel and Stange worked very closely together, of course, with Vogel having by far the more difficult job, for he could not afford to anger the party apparatus. He had to proceed with utmost discretion, a skill for which he was well known.

When the proposal to exchange Volker Heinz for Heinz Felfe was not accepted, Vogel remained undeterred. He simply forwarded his government's unambiguous threat to Bonn and waited for a response. The intense pressure worked: at stake was a second round of tough negotiations on temporary travel permits for West-Berliners. So the jockeying continued.

When I later asked Stange about the deal Vogel had suggested, he said that in his opinion it had never been about trading 'Heinz for Felfe', that quite different names had been on the list. In this matter I am rather inclined to agree with Vogel (supported by corresponding clues in the files), for why should he have lied or invented anything in my case? I regard that as highly improbable. I tend to think that Stange simply could not remember correctly.

Although I cannot conclusively prove it, I am convinced that Vogel spoke the truth, especially since he ultimately did manage to have Felfe released, just not in 1966 but a few years later, in 1969, when Brandt formed a coalition government with the FDP. In 1969 Gustav Heinemann succeeded the oft-ridiculed Heinrich Lübke as federal president. Heinemann had to sign Felfe's pardon. It is little wonder that Felfe was not set free and exchanged until then. That could not have happened under the CDU's conservative hard-liners, who totally opposed *Ostpolitik*. They would never have accepted such a pardon. In retrospect, it has become very clear to me how much the prisoner exchanges were tied to the political constellations of the day, and that a person's freedom depended on whether a politically viable moment for an exchange had presented itself. The prisoners thereby became a key economic resource within intra-German diplomacy.

* * *

'Get going,' I was told shortly after my television encounter in the Major's office. 'You're being moved to a different cell.'

Richard and I had only a few items to pack. After quickly grabbing our toothbrushes, toothpaste, plastic bowls, dictionary, pencil, and notepaper, we were ready to go. We were given no reason for being moved to a three-man cell, which was considerably larger. It was not until then that we came to appreciate how lucky we had been. Although we did not speak to each other much, we got along well. Above all, we abided by certain basic rules of coexistence. Such rapport is not to be taken for granted in prison, something I learnt when we had the misfortune of being put together with a crazy former mercenary from Dresden who had fought for the Congolese politician Moïse Tshombe and who liked spouting misogynous remarks and took sadistic pleasure in disgusting us. He bellowed when frustrated. The night he urinated on my feet, my limit was reached. I made a huge scene – and was actually heeded. The man had to leave our cell.

After the foot-fouler had gone, an Italian was assigned to our cell. I called him Giovanni. He had beautiful black hair and a rather slight build. He was extremely melancholic, for he considered himself to be an unsung poet, as he was quick to inform us. I spoke no Italian and Giovanni only broken German, so we conversed in French. Because he babbled incessantly and gesticulated extravagantly, he unquestionably enlivened our dreary life in the cell.

'Why are you here?' I asked Giovanni after he sat down at the table with us on the first day.

'Well,' he explained, 'the story's a bit complicated. As a foreigner, I entered the GDR through Checkpoint Charlie, and my hobby is to write poetry.' He always talked of '*ma poésie*'.

'But that's no crime. Something must have happened.' I became curious. Giovanni continued with a long explanation.

'I was in a pub in East Berlin and had spent the whole day working very happily on *ma poésie* – and in the evening I returned. Once over in the West, I noticed that I'd left my book with the poems in the pub. So I went back to the border official in the barrack and explained, 'I have to go back. I've left my poetry in a restaurant."

'And then they laughed at you and sent you away?'

'Exactly. How did you know?'

I shrugged my shoulders.

Giovanni continued: 'I was so enraged and unhappy about the loss that during the night I climbed to the top of the wall and came down on the other side. I had arranged for a ladder from a resident. I managed to get across the border, but I was immediately arrested.'

I was speechless. He couldn't really be serious. After I had translated the story for Richard, he stared at me: was Giovanni off his rocker? It didn't matter to us whether Giovanni had only made up this story - at least he made us laugh from time to time.

* * *

Under Chancellor Erhard, the West German government had already made efforts to free a certain number of prisoners each year. This happened in so-called annual campaigns, with the GDR not always abiding by the arrangements: such as when it did not release prisoners serving long sentences as requested but instead only prisoners with short sentences. I later learnt that I was to be included in the 1966 annual campaign, which ran from September until Christmas. By then, though, the timing was unfavourable. As a prerequisite for any release, the GDR insisted on police questioning and, in particular, criminal court proceedings, and those parts of the process had not yet been completed in my case. Recognising early on that the West German side had a particular interest in me, the GDR presumed it could sell me under better conditions, if not for Felfe, then in some other special way. Otherwise, I would have been bussed over the border in a 'group exchange' like many others. As it was, though, I was an interesting pawn and became a 'special case'. That also explains why I was sentenced to such a long prison term, which was on a par with punishments for high treason and other serious crimes. After all, the deal had to appear balanced, and the length of the prison term was easy to manipulate.

The volume of the ensuing group exchange deals is documented by Stange's letter to the Authorised Representative of the Council of the Lutheran Church in Germany, Bishop Hermann Kunst. It is one of the few published documents from that period. The letter was dated 23 November 1966:

Most Reverend Bishop Kunst,

In my letter of October 26th, 1966, I informed you that, as part of the special operation through Wartha, the other side is prepared to extend the permission to emigrate to family members of prisoners who have been released this year.

I now have the final list of this group of people. A total of 182 family members are involved. That would mean an additional sum of DM 2.1 million.

The figures relating to the other points are as follows: it is estimated that a total of 410 prisoners were planned to be released as part of the operation. These releases have taken place in all but 7 cases. These prisoners are ill so they could not be moved until now, but they will be transferred in the coming days.

In return, a sum of DM 16.4 million has been calculated.

In the area of family reunification, the emigration of 546 persons has been achieved. That comes to 21 lists at DM 300,000 each, or a total sum of DM 6.3 million.

If the other 7 lists of family reunifications and previously paid sums are included, the grand total would exceed DM 25 million.

To date, Assistant Secretary Dr. Rehlinger has given me no promise that the said 7 lists can be included. He pointed out that the amount would exceed the number considered at the beginning of the year.

Clarification is, in my opinion, only possible at a higher level.

Respectfully yours,

J Stange

The churches served as 'intermediaries' and pioneers in the intra-German prisoner exchange business. They also profited from it. Next to Vogel and Stange, Dr. Ludwig Rehlinger, reporting to minister Rainer Barzel, played an important role in the negotiations for buying out prisoners from the GDR. Barzel was soon to oppose the later *Ostpolitik* of Willy Brandt.

While I was being instructed in matters poetic by my Italian cellmate, intense discussions were already taking place in East Berlin and Bonn on how to deal with me. At that time, however, I had no inkling that these discussions were soon to yield results.

A RAY OF HOPE

In early 1967 my parents went on holiday to Bavaria's ski resort of Garmisch-Partenkirchen, an hour's drive from Munich. Vogel and Stange, who travelled often, happened to be in the Bavarian capital Munich at that time. They took the opportunity to meet there with my parents. Stange told me about this meeting after my release. My father was both tense and concerned. My mother's eyes glistened with tears most of the time. It tormented her greatly that I was in investigative custody. Vogel turned first to my father: 'Mr Heinz, negotiations concerning your son are underway.'

'Yes, I've heard or read that time and again. But I still don't know what exactly it means. Do you know anything more specific?' The waiting was wearing on my father's nerves.

'You know, of course, that is not possible. All negotiations between the FRG and the GDR of this kind are strictly confidential.'

'But no one has told me anything new for weeks now. Can't things be accelerated?' My father did not like being unable to do anything, but simply having to accept what the lawyers did or did not do.

'You must look at it this way, Mr Heinz,' Vogel explained calmly, 'Nothing can proceed before your son's trial. Without that, we cannot get him out of prison. We have to wait and see what his sentence is. Everything will be based on that. In the interest of your son, please do not initiate anything yourself.'

My father sighed and nodded. He did a lot for me – simply because he loved me despite my many escapades. Deep down he was a warm-hearted person, but he could not show it. Casting a mischievous look at Vogel and Stange, he said: 'One could get the impression that you are some kind of secret society.' Vogel smiled wryly. 'Well, you're not far off.'

'And how long will it be until my son goes on trial?'

'It usually takes five months.'

'Then it ought to be soon,' my mother chimed in hopefully.

Vogel hesitated a moment before answering. 'Unfortunately, it is likely to take a bit longer in your son's case. If he had helped only one or two GDR citizens escape, then the matter would be only half as bad. But his case involved more than sixty people, and the method included the use of a diplomat. That is a totally different dimension which cannot simply be dismissed as though it were only a silly boyish prank. There is a complete list of all entry and exit dates.'

My mother's eyes filled with tears again.

'Is it personally or socially hard for you to deal with the fact that you son is in jail?' Stange ventured to ask.

My father shook his head vigorously. 'Not socially, more personally. Look at my wife. And Volker's three siblings are suffering quietly. To me, his helping people escape is an extension of his fearless disposition, to which he likes succumbing without regard for his family.'

My mother contradicted him with surprising vehemence, but she was actually only doing what she always did – defend me.

'No, to me he is a hero! He has helped so many people gain freedom.'

My father wordlessly looked up to the ceiling, as though wishing to signal that no one understood him properly anyway. Vogel left with the words, 'Believe me, we've brought you good news.'

My father did not have to pay for my release. It was the West German government that paid, but I never found out exactly how much. The commerce in freedom had in fact taken on impressive dimensions. Between 1963 and 1989 a total of 33,755 political prisoners were granted early release from detention. Over those twenty-six years, the West German government paid approximately DM 3.5 billion, the equivalent of about €100,000 (currently US$114,000) per person. At first the sums were negotiated individually, but after the exchanges had developed into a mass business, it quickly became clear that it was impossible to negotiate anew each time. A standard price was eventually agreed from which deviations were made in special cases – usually upwards. Vogel indicated to me later that the price for my release, in addition to the exchange for two KGB spies, was significantly higher than the normal rate. But I have been unable to find out anything more about it.

* * *

It was March 1967. First, Richard disappeared from the cell, followed a short time thereafter by Giovanni. I never saw either of them again. I was put into a one-man cell, which was not entirely unwelcome to me. I had gradually gained control over my depression, but, of course, it was still painful to imagine how much time still lay before me. I had not expected to wait six months for the first meeting with a lawyer, but at last I briefly conferred with Wolfgang Vogel. A second meeting took place in early June. In both instances I was brought to Magdalenenstrasse in one of the prisoner-transport vans.

A lawyer, I thought enthusiastically. Finally, a lawyer, a man with whom I can calmly discuss everything. My heart was bursting with joy as I sat in the windowless vehicle in eager anticipation of my first open conversation in six months. Once inside the Magdalenenstrasse detention facility, I was led into one of the typically bare rooms to which I had become quite accustomed.

'Sit down at the table,' ordered a warder, pointing ostentatiously to a chair. A second chair stood on the other side. It was still unoccupied.

'Where is he?' I asked.

'Wait.'

The warder remained standing at the door, not taking his eyes off me for a second. My whole body felt his piercing gaze.

'Hands on the table,' he ordered.

Was this a ploy? Was something quite different going on here? I mentally prepared myself for the possibility that the meeting with the lawyer was only a pretext. Maybe an attempt to recruit me as an agent would now follow, with methods more brutal than those the Major had employed – if that had been his intent.

I looked around me. The walls were a yellowish brown, the same colour as in Hohenschönhausen. Except for the table and the two chairs, it was completely bare. Eerily so. I stared at the table, with its dirty-grey laminated surface. Then there was a knock on the cell door. The jailer rattled his keyring. As the door opened, I saw from the corner of my eye a somewhat stocky man about 1.75 metres tall (5 foot 7) with a finely etched face and wearing a large pair of glasses. His hair was already thinning around the crown. He was wearing a good-quality suit and a perfectly knotted tie. Tucked under his arm was a briefcase, which was amazingly thin. He had few papers with him. Nevertheless, he could not be working for the Stasi. He looked entirely like one imagines a lawyer to look. I estimated him to be about twenty years older than me (not a bad guess, as I found out later he was 18 years my senior). Overall, he immediately made a positive impression on me. Rather a quiet person.

With the warder behind him, Vogel entered the visitors' room with his finger to his lips, directing his eyes to the ceiling. Of course. The room was bugged. Why hadn't I thought of that? A wave of disappointment washed over me. I could forget about having an open conversation, yet I had so many questions. But I had to keep silent as he had clearly indicated.

'Good afternoon. Are you my lawyer?' I greeted him.

'Yes,' Vogel confirmed. He had a kind, pleasant voice. 'My name is Vogel, and you are Volker Heinz?'

I nodded.

In terms of due process, the situation was obviously dubious because Wolfgang Vogel played several roles simultaneously. He not only represented me as my lawyer, he also served the state that had brought criminal charges against me. In this capacity he was a purveyor of political prisoners. Bluntly put, he delivered humanitarian relief in exchange for West German treasure. But the times and circumstances were exceptional. When Wolfgang Vogel died in 2008, the obituary that ran in the *Frankfurter Allgemeine*

Zeitung stated that he 'was one of the few people during the Cold War who could make the dream of freedom become reality. He was the final hope for many people seeking to emigrate from the GDR, including a number of spies.' I agree with this assessment and always defended him when anyone found his dealings unethical or portrayed him as a 'pivotal figure of modern human trafficking' (*Die Welt*), or as an *Advocatus Diaboli* (Craig Whitney of the *New York Times*).

Vogel had been working in East Berlin since qualifying as a lawyer. Three years later he had also obtained the right to practise law in West Berlin. That was possible in the 1950s since the statutory law, especially civil law, was still largely the same in both parts of Germany. Beginning in 1963, he negotiated the release of some 33,000 prisoners from GDR prisons with West German Government representatives including Jürgen Stange. Furthermore, he arranged for the resettlement of more than 250,000 East German citizens to the West. Some 150 spies are said to have been exchanged. In 1985 Vogel (like Felfe) received a professorship at the SED's institution for training political activists or cadres at the University of Law and Administration in Golm near Potsdam. After the collapse of the Communist regime, he was accused of having pressured East German emigrants into selling their houses to exalted members of the party. His acquittal was welcomed by his friends and admirers with great joy and relief.

Our meeting lasted ten minutes at most. Vogel informed me when the trial was scheduled to begin. It was still several months off, so the news was not exactly joyous.

'And what then?' I asked, somewhat demoralised.

'Well, you can expect a long prison sentence,' he answered sombrely. 'I'll try to come to the trial myself, but I may well have to send my colleague, Dr Berg. However, there is hope.'

My eyes lit up. 'What kind of hope?'

Vogel again placed his finger on his lips. 'I can't tell you,' he whispered. 'And you have not heard what I just said, OK?'

* * *

I spent the next few weeks secluded in my cell. I read a lot, learned more Russian vocabulary, ran as much as possible in the exercise cage. If gloomy thoughts overwhelmed me, I blocked the menace of depression. *However, there is hope.* Remembering this one sentence lifted my spirits and made the isolation easier to bear. It wasn't until a good two months later, in early June, that the second meeting with Vogel took place, in the same building and the same room.

'Your trial is in two or three weeks,' Vogel said. Again, he made a cryptic remark that to me nevertheless sounded like good news: 'We're making great progress. Things are about to start moving.'

That could have meant just about anything. But I only wanted to hear positive news, so to me 'great progress' could only mean something good. I was certain that it was a coded message intended to tell me that I would have to appear in court, but that we had something within our grasp. Just what, however, I didn't know.

I did not gain any further information from this conversation. Again, we had to assume that we were being listened in on. After a short while Vogel left the room, and I was handcuffed, led to the windowless prisoner van, and taken back to Hohenschönhausen. The days before the trial became endlessly long. Hadn't four weeks already passed since I last saw Vogel? No, it just seemed that way to me. It had been only seven days. Time was the worst enemy in the cell.

Meanwhile, things were also advancing in Bonn. The person for whom I was to be exchanged had been determined. In a letter to Assistant Secretary Dr. Rehlinger on 16 June 1967, Stange informed the West German government: 'If a pardon is granted to Clemens, who is serving time in the Bochum prison, the GDR has declared itself prepared to release the student Volker Heinz by the end of July at the latest.' In a way, my case was therefore being linked with Heinz Felfe after all. Hans Clemens was Felfe's close associate and, like Felfe, a KGB spy. He had received a ten-year prison sentence. In a letter to Jürgen Stange dated 20 June, Vogel explained the GDR's position:

We have negotiated the matter several times. I have now been expressly authorised to inform you:

1. Mr Heinz shall be released in the first half of July and sent to West Berlin or the German Federal Republic (at your discretion) on the condition that Mr Hans Max Clemens is released at the latest concurrently. I assume it will be possible for me to speak with Mr Clemens a day before his release in order to clarify where he would like to take up residence. In cases such as these, you, dear colleague, likewise have the opportunity for such a discussion in a prison here.

2. The fifteen accomplices already known to you from Mr Heinz's dossier shall be released in the course of the 1967 operation. Most of the proceedings have not yet been concluded.

3. My side declares its consent solely because this arrangement should lend itself to facilitating a mutually acceptable solution to the Felfe case before the end of 1967. I do not wish to withhold from you that my side originally intended to consider

the Heinz case and the accomplices only in connection with the Felfe case. On the basis of my letter today, may the willingness to engage not be misinterpreted but rather recognised. Mr Heinz's trial will take place on 27 June 1967 before the municipal court of Greater Berlin, Littenstrasse Courthouse, room 395. Media coverage is not foreseen. The matter is very complex. More than 30 persons were successfully smuggled. There were diplomatic entanglements. The 'special efforts' undertaken by the FRG will have no bearing on the sentencing of Mr. Heinz by the court, whether or not agreement on his release can be reached. Since the pardoning of Mr Heinz must be decided by the Chairman of the Council of State [Walter Ulbricht], preparatory time of ten days is required. I therefore request your immediate reply.

Without my having the faintest idea of what was going on, German-German strings were secretly being pulled. Clemens and another KGB spy were exchanged for me. To this day I do not know the name of the second spy. But in this deal, as in many others, it is interesting to note that the GDR was used by the Soviet Union for its own purposes. After all, Clemens and Felfe were not Stasi, but KGB spies!

THE MOCK TRIAL

'Volker Heinz was lured into helping people escape. He became an instrument of the enemies of our State of Workers and Farmers…' Thus Vogel's colleague, Dr Berg, defended me during the court proceedings on 27 June 1967. Berg was an elderly, grey-haired gentleman in an oversized grey suit. He genuinely tried to cast a better light on the long list of my escape operations. But what could he say in my defence? I had committed a crime, politically just about the worst one possible in the GDR. It was a depressing affair.

According to the indictment, I was appearing before the court because of 'inducement to leave the GDR' as defined in section 21, subsection 1 of the East German Criminal Law Supplementation Act. That sounded quite harmless. But it was anything but harmless. My behaviour was termed 'inducement' or enticement: the MfS wanted to make the point that people from the West, like me, were the aggressors, and that the people of the GDR had no interest whatsoever in leaving their own country. After 1968, the offence for which I was now standing trial no longer existed. It was reworded, and as a result sounded more modern (and more bureaucratic). I would have been accused of 'aiding and abetting the unlawful crossing of the border'.

Few people today remember that the GDR long applied the same laws and regulations as the FRG. The country simply lacked the time and energy to develop its own socialist penal code, so it was formally decided to incorporate section 21 into the East German Criminal Law Supplementation Act. Older lawyers such as Vogel had been forced to adapt. It was only after the construction of the Wall and the ensuing internal political consolidation that the GDR gradually developed its own criminal code.

The trial took place in central Berlin (Berlin-Mitte) in what is now the regional court on Littenstrasse. At the time of my trial, this late nineteenth-century imperial building – with its idiosyncratic blend of Neo-Baroque, Art Nouveau, and Gothic – housed the Supreme Court, the offices of the Prosecutor-General of the GDR, and the Municipal Court of Greater Berlin. The street was named after Hans Litten, a courageous defence lawyer for the proletariat and an opponent of the National Socialists. Early on, in 1933, the Nazis took him into 'protective custody' and deported him to various concentration camps. After being tortured many times in Dachau concentration camp, he committed suicide in 1938.

I was brought to the courthouse in a car that resembled a bloated Trabant, the much maligned Trabi, the 'spark plug with a roof'. Compared to the prison's other transport vehicles, it was comfortable. Nevertheless, I felt confined. I estimated that the drive did not last longer than twenty minutes. The trial was to begin at 8:30 am.

The main entrance was so vast that every defendant who walked through it was bound to feel overwhelmed. However,

I was led through one of the two side entrances. Two jailers escorted me into an imposing hall from which various flights of stairs ascended to the upper floors. I climbed the stairs accompanied by both men, but I was not handcuffed. That would have been completely unnecessary: the court building had armed, uniformed guards posted everywhere.

I wore my prison attire. I had actually expected at least a modicum of respect, hoping that my civilian clothing would be returned to me for the trial. This did not happen.

In 1992, some twenty-five years later, and three years after the fall of the Wall, I moved back to now re-unified Berlin. I had meanwhile qualified as a German attorney in 1973 and as an English barrister in 1990, subsequently working in London for a number of years. My first civil case took place in precisely the same, still un-renovated courthouse where I had once appeared in prison attire, accused of a serious crime. Clad in my German lawyer's robe, I found it overpowering to walk through the very place where I had stood before the court myself. It took ten to fifteen years before I lost this peculiar feeling, which I ascribed to 'after effects', like sleeping with an arm over my eyes, the habit I had developed in my prison cell. After a seemingly infinite number of stairs, we reached the third floor, and I entered courtroom number 395.

'Sit next to your lawyer,' someone ordered, directing me to the elderly gentleman in grey.

So Vogel couldn't come personally, I thought to myself. A pity. Berg was one of the reserve lawyers whom Vogel employed to take on relatively small assignments, or, as in my case, to step in for a colleague. But it was also possible that Vogel had arranged for a deputy because he knew that criminal proceedings of this nature were won in the political arena, not in the courtroom.

Dr Berg shook my hand. 'You know that you'll be convicted?' he whispered.

'Yes,' I answered.

'I cannot do much for you.'

'That's clear to me. You can hardly seek an acquittal,' I added with a tired smile.

'You are not blameless,' he explained, lowering his voice even more. 'Everything I say here serves only the goal of achieving a lenient sentence. I will therefore only present extenuating circumstances by stressing that you confessed and that you have not been obstructive.'

'I assume that you have coordinated the defence strategy with Dr Vogel,' I said, immediately realising that his plea would be brief. Indeed, that is exactly how it turned out. He sounded rather shy, quiet, and entreating. His was not an especially persuasive plea. But it did not bother me. I was anyway only counting on Vogel's earlier careful remarks.

Everyone rose as the three judges entered. The presiding judge was probably at least sixty years old. He had to be a staunch party loyalist to hold such an important position. He took his seat between two lay assessors: a brunette in her forties, who was a lathe operator by training, and an industrial manager in his fifties who had blond, very short hair. Neither said a single word during the proceedings, asked no questions, and only kept shaking their heads gravely. No, really, how could anyone dare smuggle people out of their 'workers' paradise'?

However, the judge presiding over my trial was only a pawn himself. He merely did what he had to do. The key people were the public prosecutor and a man representing the MfS. In my court records, I later found the ministry's remark on the sentence it would 'recommend' the prosecutor to plead. When the MfS recommended something, it was not advisable to plead for a lighter punishment - especially if one wanted a career as a public prosecutor. As a young woman in her thirties, this was precisely the impression the prosecutor made. It was obvious that every verdict against a political prisoner was a political verdict and that the sentence was a political sentence.

The trial began. My personal information was verified, the charge was read aloud, and the judge asked a few questions. Everything proceeded in a relatively benign fashion, and at first the hearing appeared dry and uneventful. My confession, it was stressed, had established that I had joined the Fuchs smuggling organisation in December 1965 and that by September 1966 I had participated in smuggling more than sixty people at the behest of this organisation. It was stated that I had not entered into contact with either US intelligence agencies or the employees of the Syrian consulate and that I had not taken money for my activities. It was also noted that all the people I had smuggled had been chosen by the Fuchs organisation, except for the physician's family whose escape I had initiated. The charge continued that the people whom I had hidden in the boot of the car included two physicians and twelve engineers. That was, so to speak, the 'macroeconomic damage' I had inflicted. Everything went very much as I had expected. But then something unusual happened. The judge presented me with a photograph.

'Do you know this man?'

How often had I already been asked that question? How often had I been shown this picture? Once again, it was the one of Heiko Neumann.

'No, I don't know him,' I replied. On innumerable previous occasions I had denied knowing this escape helper. I wanted to stick to that story.

'You really don't?' repeated the judge incredulously.

'As I have often said, this man is unknown to me.'

With a wave of the judge's hand, the door to the chamber opened, and I stared in disbelief as Heiko Neumann was led in.

'Do you know the accused, Volker Heinz?' asked the judge, turning to Heiko Neumann with a victorious grin.

'Yes,' answered Neumann, but said nothing more.

While Heiko was being led back out of the chamber, the next question was obvious: 'And do you now know Heiko Neumann? Or do you wish to stand by your statement?'

It was a somewhat surreal scene reminiscent of the night in Magdalenenstrasse, when Kamal and the married couple were presented to me. Resigned, I answered: 'I no longer see the need to deny it.'

Who could have helped me in this situation? Perhaps Berg could have attempted to justify my previous denials and plead some kind of understanding, but he was evidently just as unprepared for this turn of events as I.

Six years after my release, I saw Heiko Neumann again by chance. He was sitting alone in a restaurant in Berlin, so I took a seat at his table. I have no idea why I did that, but it seemed absurd for me to ignore him. We recognised each other immediately, of course. At first, neither of us knew what to say. We were embarrassed because both of us felt guilty: Heiko, because he had revealed that he knew me; I, because, unlike me, he had served the full five-year sentence he had been given. Only a year before this chance encounter had he been released.

'I'm sorry,' I finally said.

'So am I,' came his immediate reply.

'According to my sense of justice, there was no reason not to buy your freedom.'

Heiko merely shrugged his shoulders. I could tell how painful it all still was for him. The West German government had declined to buy him back earlier because he had committed an unrelated minor crime under the law as it stood then. In my opinion neither the verdict nor the fact that he had been forced to serve his entire, long sentence was commensurate. We parted in sadness and never saw each other again.

After Dr Berg's brief plea, the bench withdrew for consultation. I knew that the scene with Neumann had undermined my lawyer's portrayal of me as having been cooperative. The minutes that passed until the verdict was read out seemed like an eternity.

'How long will it take?' I asked Dr Berg.

'Twenty minutes at most in my experience.'

'Twenty minutes can be a long time.'

Dr Berg agreed and then said, 'I'd like to advise you not to appeal. That would only unnecessarily delay things.'

I began to wonder. What did he mean by 'delay'? For the first time I allowed myself to consider that he might be referring to my early release. Of course, I could not speak openly and said only, 'You've no doubt consulted with Mr Vogel about this?'

'Yes, exactly.' Dr Berg gave me a knowing look.

The judge and the two lay assessors re-entered the courtroom. I rose for the pronouncement of the verdict 'in the name of the people'. Neumann was not to be the only surprise in this trial. Vogel had indicated that I would receive a fairly long prison sentence, but what followed was nevertheless still a shock. Due to 'continued inducement to leave the German Democratic Republic illegally as defined by section 21, subsection 1, number 1 of the Criminal Law Supplementation Act', I was sentenced to twelve years in prison.

Twelve years? I would have liked to sit down, but the judge still had several items to read. I was stunned. I had reckoned with ten years at the very most; now it was twelve. That was half of my life so far, and it was to be spent behind bars. Automatically, I began to calculate. I would be able to resume my studies at the age of 36. Was I dreaming? Stop. I pulled myself together at once. Stay calm, don't think too much. I literally clung to Vogel's words, to his intimations. It just couldn't be that I was mistaken.

When the judge had finished, Dr Berg informed him that I expressly waived my right to appeal. The trial was over. It had lasted one and a half hours. One big farce. Not a single one of 'my' escapees had been identified by name. There had been just as little mention of GDR citizens and their yearning for freedom as there had been of my wish to help them. There had been nothing but ideological platitudes.

After the sentence had been read out, I was returned to my cell. Everything happened as in a film viewed in fast-forward mode. Before long, I was back in the gated area of the prison. Routine! Routine! Routine! The word buzzed incessantly in my head. The entire proceedings had been pure routine, a kind of show trial without the public. A secret event behind closed doors. How much fear the GDR must have felt to shun the presence of its own citizens! I hadn't been so upset for a long time and sought to vent my rage, tension, and disillusionment. But at whom should I direct these feelings? The warders? The Major? The lieutenant? No, surely not. Not a scream, not a curse passed my lips. Not once did I even clench my fists. I focused all my thoughts on Vogel's words.

ATTEMPTS TO RECRUIT

Meanwhile, prisoner transactions between Bonn and East Berlin continued unremittingly. Just one day after my trial, West-Germany's Permanent Under-Secretary of State, Carl Krautwig, reported to Herbert Wehner, the Federal Minister for All-German Affairs:

On Tuesday, June 27th, 1967, I consulted with the representatives of both the Protestant and Catholic Churches, Bishop Kunst and Auxiliary Bishop Tenhumberg. We discussed the proposal that the GDR-attorney-at-law Vogel had submitted to the two churches through his Western colleague Stange: to continue the so-called prisoner operation. This proposal provides for the exchange of prisoners, including those with both short or long sentences, in order to reunite families and to repatriate children. If the proposal were to be accepted by the other side, DM 40 million [about US$10 million at that time] would be due from our side. The other side regards its proposal as a take-it-or-leave-it package... The West German intelligence agents still serving time in the GDR are not included in this proposal. According to the explanation by attorney-at-law Vogel, those cases can be resolved only in conjunction with the settling of the Felfe case.

I was sitting at the wooden table in my cell, as I did every day, learning Russian vocabulary. But I could barely concentrate.

As I looked up from my notebook and stared at the familiar pattern of glass bricks, I asked myself why nothing was happening. Two weeks had passed since my trial, and there had been nothing to indicate that I had interpreted Vogel's words correctly. What on earth was the matter? Had I deceived myself? Had I naïvely clutched at a hope that did not exist? Terrible doubts assailed me, I felt my throat tightening. I had woken up sweating profusely in recent nights, trying repeatedly to remember the exact wording, syllable for syllable. I had often trusted my instincts in life – had I now met my doom? No, it couldn't be. I went to great lengths to banish the thought completely.

Yet, as though wanting to be convinced of my plight, I sometimes told myself, 'Volker, accept it. It simply didn't work out.' Nevertheless, I just couldn't content myself with this conclusion. I couldn't and wouldn't acknowledge it. My impatience seemed to have climaxed. I longed so much to be able to take my own decisions again. Why was I not receiving news? Why was I being left in such uncertainty?

Suddenly, a startling thought shot through my mind. What if I were not allowed to acquire any kind of training during twelve years of imprisonment? What if they were to send me to slave away in a mine? I could also be assigned to do the dirty work in a chemical factory. Richard had told me that nearly all economic sectors of the workers' and farmers' state profited from the work done by inmates. He had also mentioned that some were even carted off to work in the uranium mine and labour camp near 'Wismut' (a code name for mining facilities in Thuringia and Saxony from which the Soviet Union drew raw materials for its nuclear industry). But a person would survive there only five or six years at most. By that point you'd be more or less dead, not because of the hard labour but because of the radiation. As I dwelt on my sinister thoughts, the keys turned in the massive lock of my cell door. That was not a matter of routine.

Raising my eyes, I saw two men standing in the doorway. They almost looked like the men in the leather jackets. Not until they approached me was I able to make out their faces clearly. They were in their late thirties, early forties, and were definitely Stasi officers. They looked bright and alert as they scrutinised the cell.

Confined to a one-man cell, I had no visitors' chairs to offer them, so I rose from my stool – also in order to be at eye level with them. My pulse soared. What did they want from me? Every possible thought raced through my head, including the fear that they may want to beat or torture me. But no, I was mistaken. Their greeting was positively friendly.

'Good afternoon, Mr Heinz. Excuse us for dropping by unannounced. You presumably do not know us?'

Friendly torturers? Rather unlikely. I relaxed a little. 'No, I haven't as yet had that honour.'

'Fine, fine.'

'Is there a particular reason for your visit?' I inquired. I did not want to give the impression of being too afraid.

'Well,' the younger of the two men began cautiously, 'we have a certain interest...'

All at once, I understood: They were the ones who had wanted to jump into the moving S-Bahn carriage. And now they hoped to recruit me as their agent in the West before I left the GDR. I started breathing more slowly again. Their surprise visit calmed me down considerably, for it basically confirmed my suspicion that some sort of strings were being pulled in the background to secure my release. The appearance of the two men could only mean that it was to happen soon, that I – I scarcely dared imagine it – would soon be a free man again.

I had often wondered why a person first had to be convicted in order to be set free, why no one was ever released beforehand while the case was still under investigation. But now I understood: Exploit every opportunity to squeeze the lemon as much as possible. For a state critically short of hard currency, the idea was to extract the very last drop. Hence the necessity of a conviction and a heavy penalty. Had anyone held in custody pending trial ever been released from Hohenschönhausen? That would have meant confessing to a mistake. And that was about as preposterous as tearing down the Wall.

There was an exception, however, as I later found out: Ulrike Poppe, the Regional Commissioner for the Appraisal of the Consequences of the Communist Dictatorship in Brandenburg. In 1983 she was arrested on 'suspicion of treasonous communication' and brought to Hohenschönhausen, but she was set free after just six weeks because her detention triggered massive protests in both her own country and abroad. But in the 1960s, something like that was inconceivable.

I did not have to wait long for an explanation from my visitors.

'You know Wolfgang Fuchs, The Tunnel Fox,' began the older man.

Aha! That's the way the wind is blowing. Fuchs.

'Yes, I know him,' I said. 'It's in the interrogation transcripts.'

'You can perhaps imagine,' remarked the younger one, 'that we want to put an end to his game.'

I did not intend to oblige.

'And what does that have to do with me?' I asked naïvely.

'I think you know exactly,' the older man said, his voice sharpening a little. 'He's putting many innocent people into the line of fire. You're one of his victims, too, and that's why we can imagine that you have an interest in seeing it end, as do we.'

'Aha,' I said noncommittally. Because I could not precisely gauge how this conversation would develop, I had to keep a door open. So I feigned acceptance of possible cooperation but kept myself covered. 'You know,' I continued, 'after what I have been through here, you can be sure that I've thought critically about my activities. Because I am not yet free, I cannot say at this point whether I'm primarily interested in entering your services. You can't expect that of me at the moment.'

'We understand that, but...'

'But,' I interrupted, 'I don't want to completely exclude it, either. I just have to collect my thoughts first. My biggest concern, if I were free again, would be to finish my studies.'

'We understand that, too. Nonetheless, we'd like to give you an address so that you can contact us at any time. Is that all right with you?'

Incredible, this false courtesy. 'Naturally,' I replied with equally feigned politeness. I hoped that I had given a satisfactory answer. I did not mention that cooperation was, of course, utterly out of the question for me. I did not think a clear no would have been wise in this situation. What if it were to delay or even prevent my release? My release. What was I thinking? Not a word had been said about release yet. Why was I taking it for granted? Wouldn't it be better gradually to warm up to the idea of sanding down chair legs or gluing countless shoes together day after day with the other prisoners?

Supremely trained in handling absurd situations such as this, the two visitors responded, 'We see that you have paper and pencil. Please note down the following address.'

I took the paper and pencil, and the younger man dictated a street name and an East Berlin postal code. No secret cipher. No encryption. Nothing. A completely normal postal address. I could hardly believe it. He added, 'Well, when you've thought it over and are ready to turn to us – you have the information.'

With that, the visit ended. It had lasted no longer than ten minutes.

'Good-bye, Mr Heinz,' the younger man said. 'All the best to you. It would be nice if you could help us.'

'Yes, we would welcome it and would reciprocate if we hear from you,' the man with him said. Then the cell door was closed and locked behind them.

I sat perplexed on my chair, trying to digest this bizarre encounter. Not a trace of aggression. They had neither gloated nor implored. They had pulled no paper from their pockets for me to sign. I had not had to commit myself to anything. But even if they had used thumbscrews on me, I would not have given them a single signature. I had already signed a sufficient number of interrogation records. Enough was enough. Moreover, *they* acted like the ones needing help. Rather clever. These Stasi people were no fools. Their organisation was justifiably considered among the world's best intelligence services. And what surprised me the most was how respectfully they had treated me.

So they were going after Wolfgang Fuchs, I mused. Well, they can wait a long time for that. Never in my life would I think of betraying him. His involvement in helping people escape impressed me, and that had not changed during my time in prison.

The two Stasi men may not have been aware that they had really done me a favour with their visit. It seemed more plausible than ever to me that I would be released. Indeed, that's what it *had* to mean, for what was I to do with a Stasi address in an East German jail? Wasn't that great news! I was now convinced that my instincts had not deceived me.

Forgetting about the dictionary and notebook, I looked around my cell feverishly. Would I still spend a night on the wooden plank bed, or would everything get underway this very day? Composed, I sat there and waited. My capacity for self-control had helped me from the outset. Of course, it had not prevented depression, but it did help me endure my detention. I sensed that I only had to hold out a little longer.

It had been important to me to pay attention to all the details around me and go about things as an alert detective would. I believed that my strategy of confessing only what would not endanger anyone else had succeeded. Of course, I could have refused to cooperate at all. East German citizens who hated the system often did that. It was out of the question for them ever to expose themselves, even partially. Ultimately, they were intent on protecting their immediate and wider social network. What an enormous strain it must have been to deny everything again and again. I had experienced it first-hand, albeit to a much lesser degree. It had become increasingly difficult for me, too, because Bergmann kept probing, knowing all too well how to weaken a person psychologically. I had constantly asked myself: what did they really know that I did not?

Lying on my wooden plank bed that night, I had only one thought: It's about to happen!

EXCHANGE IN HERLESHAUSEN

It was 11 July 1967. The cell door opened, breaking routine once again. It was the very day after the Stasi officers' visit.

'Mr Heinz, you can go and collect your things,' the jailer said.

There it was – the sentence for which I had been waiting so long. The jailer uttered it as mundanely as if he were informing me that instead of lentil stew we were having carrot stew today. Whereas he remained completely impassive (after all, this was not about his release), I was completely overwhelmed. The excitement even made me forget my Russian notes, just as the Italian had left behind his '*poesie*' in an East Berlin pub.

A uniformed officer led me to the room in which prisoners' personal effects were stored. He walked at a measured pace; I followed him, scarcely able to suppress my joy. I did not want to jeopardise anything on this last stretch, so I tried hard to feign indifference. In the storeroom everything was returned to me that I had deposited there nearly a year earlier, including my matches and a handkerchief. Nothing was missing. There must be order!

'May I put on my own clothes again?' I asked cautiously.

'That's why you're here,' came the terse reply.

The trousers still fitted; so did the shirt and jacket. Perhaps they were all a bit looser than when I had first arrived, but not really noticeably so. The clothes smelled rather musty. I doubt they had been washed or dry cleaned during the preceding ten months.

'Here, you mustn't forget this,' said a third uniformed man, handing me a piece of paper.

'What is it?' I asked.

'Your certificate of release.'

There they were, the three words that allowed me to breathe a deep sigh of relief and provided me with certainty at last.

'Thank you very much.' Taking the document as carefully as a diamond, I put it into the pocket of my jacket.

'Well, come along then. I'll take you to the gates.'

Once again I stood at the heavy iron sliding gate, it felt like being in a film. Another jailer pulled out his heavy keyring and unlocked it. Suddenly it occurred to me that I had not said goodbye to Lieutenant Bergmann. But I could deal with that, as, no doubt, could he.

Parked on the other side of the gate, in the courtyard, was one of the prisoner transport vans with which I had become quite familiar. 'Eat more fresh fish!' or something of that nature was painted on it.

Next to the van I discovered a different vehicle, which was conspicuous in this setting. It was a spacious dark-blue BMW. I looked at its registration plate, wondering whether it came from West Germany. But no, it was from the GDR. The driver stood next to the car as though rooted to the ground. He wore a grey suit and a cap, both of which looked a little rumpled.

'Get in,' he ordered.

'With pleasure,' I answered. 'But where are we going?' I tried to draw him into conversation, but he insisted on remaining silent. This behaviour would not change over the next four or five hours, either. It did not matter; I had my certificate of release in my pocket, so nothing was likely to go wrong any more.

I chose to sit in the back, not behind the mute driver but on the right with an unencumbered view ahead. (There were no headrests to block the view in those days.) The uniformed man who had taken me to the inner gate pressed a button, and the heavy iron outer gate screeched as it rolled open. The jailer, too, wasted no time on goodbyes. The whole scene somehow reminded me of a funeral, except that I was in the best of moods.

Through the BMW's large windows, I was able to see the prison compound from the outside for the first time. We turned right onto a short street lined on the right side by a series of workshop barracks. On the left stood a large brick building. It appeared to be some kind of administrative building. After the fall of the Wall, the prison complex at Hohenschönhausen was declared a national memorial. As I learnt on a subsequent visit, the building had originally been erected as a large kitchen for the National Socialist Public Welfare programme. The Soviets subsequently turned the facility into 'Special Camp 3'. In the 1950s, the GDR's Wild West period, many physicians, radio employees, and actors such as Heinrich George were imprisoned there. Most of them were victims of denunciations. The cellars were converted by the inmates into a subterranean block of damp, cold, and windowless cells furnished only with a wooden plank bed and a wooden bucket. This area was called the 'submarine' because the prisoners there felt so confined. These dungeons contained water cells, standing and crouching cells (spaces so confining that the occupant could only remain erect or else squat), and other torture cells, all intended to break the prisoners' resistance. My cells were located in the modern, three-story, U-shaped building that had been finished in 1961. Its completion led to the closure of the subterranean jail.

I was later to visit the entire complex several times. This formerly restricted zone continued to haunt me. I learned that the people living in the immediate vicinity of Genslerstrasse knew what was happening inside the compound. Most of them worked for the Stasi anyway. I once had a conversation with an elderly married couple who still lived there. They told me they had not been operatives for the MfS but had learned of what was going on behind the walls. They had been forbidden to talk about it and were threatened with criminal prosecution if they did.

After passing the main building, we turned left and then immediately right, bringing us to a large iron gate. It, too, was electrically operated. It slowly rolled aside. A fabulously sunny day lay before me and the prison walls were finally behind me.

'Isn't the weather glorious?' I said with irrepressible joy as I saw leaves, trees, and small, wispy clouds in the radiant blue sky. As we drove past houses, I saw people going about their daily business: standing in their small front gardens, cleaning windows, pushing baby carriages. I soaked everything up, every detail of normal life that I had not seen for nearly a year. I had completely forgotten how magnificent even the most trivial things were. Never again will I forget this joy, this happiness. All the women walking down the streets in their summer dresses seemed like beauty queens to me. My excellent mood was improving by the minute.

'Isn't it glorious?' I repeated.

The driver said not a word. He refused to be drawn into conversation.

Despite my enthusiasm for the world around me, I instinctively noted every turn the silent chauffeur took, every single street sign. We did not turn right onto Landsberger Allee but left, and continued through outskirts of the city that I did not know, travelling to a north-south motorway that was new to me. My day visa had always only covered the metropolitan area, so these surroundings here were unfamiliar. Today I know that we took the Berlin Ring road towards Leipzig, our destination being the border crossing at Wartha/Herleshausen. This was the frontier between the East German state of Thuringia and the West German state of Hesse. Because I held a West German rather than a West Berlin identity card, I was not simply taken to West Berlin through a Berlin border crossing but instead all the way to the Federal Republic. The GDR distinguished meticulously between the two western political units.

We drove through beautiful summer landscapes in full bloom. It was simply overwhelming. A strange feeling overcame me. Soon I would return to my normal life again. In the previous eleven months I had only had very little contact with other people. If I had been in the penitentiary, I would certainly have met other inmates and learned of their fates, but prisoners in Hohenschönhausen were isolated. How do you pick up where you left off? I had no idea.

After driving for about four hours, we stopped at a roadside parking lot. Two men were waiting there, one of whom I recognised: Wolfgang Vogel. The other man looked considerably older. He could have been in his mid-fifties.

'Good afternoon, Mr Heinz. Please get into my car now,' said Vogel, pointing to a large metallic gold Mercedes. As I later found out, I had been brought to this place in the second man's car.

He was waiting for my arrival in order to return to East Berlin with two KGB spies who were being released in exchange for me.

Vogel's gold-coloured limousine astonished me. Whoever drove a car with such a striking colour had to possess a good deal of vanity and enjoyed the luxuries of life. Years later, he told me that he owned a villa directly on Lake Teupitz in Mark Brandenburg, where many of his key negotiations had taken place. After the opening of the East–West border in 1989 and the collapse of the communist regime, he was arrested on the estate on suspicion of extortion and tax evasion. Following his release from prison, he moved to Schliersee in Upper Bavaria, where he no longer felt confronted by his GDR past.

'Who was that man?' I asked Vogel.

'Prosecutor-General Josef Streit,' he replied.

'Aha,' was my only response.

The mute driver had already taken his seat at the steering wheel of the BMW, and the prosecutor-general now sat in my place. The engine started. I was deep in thought as I watched the car drive away. How strange it must have been for the chauffeur to be forbidden to communicate with his passengers. He drove off to pick up the two spies, including Felfe's accomplice, Clemens, without me witnessing any part of the transaction.

'We're now driving to the Herleshausen border-crossing,' Vogel said as his Mercedes rolled onto the autobahn.

I was bursting to ask what had led to my release. But I did not dare pose that question. A dark-blue BMW, a gold coloured Mercedes, how ostentatious! Vogel had come personally, and the prosecutor-general certainly belonged to the East German political elite.

'Your parents are waiting for you on the other side of the border.'

I hadn't expected that. I had assumed I would board a train alone and travel to – well, who knows where? My parents had surely given up my apartment in Bonn. I could have gone to Wuppertal, giving me a number of hours to prepare myself for meeting my parents in familiar surroundings. But my surprise was quickly eclipsed by the even greater joy of anticipation.

Vogel announced that we would also see someone else on the other side of the border – my West German lawyer, Jürgen Stange, whom I had never met before.

'We still have some business to take care of,' Vogel explained with an enigmatic smile. I didn't ask any questions.

And then we arrived in Herleshausen. The border gate opened. My parents were standing there, my mother with tears streaming down her face, beside her my father with a relieved but cautious smile. Behind them I could see my father's chauffeur, who was taking photos. My mother, in light summer attire, embraced me tightly, not wanting to let me go. Then my father, too, briefly took me into his arms. We were not capable of saying more to each other than 'How good to have you back,' and 'Thank you so much for coming to pick me up.'

Vogel and Stange remained in the background. I managed to thank them briefly and say good-bye. The photographs taken by the chauffeur show both men only from a distance as they prepared to make their way back to the GDR and West Berlin, respectively. I felt liberated, overjoyed, and grateful. I still could not really believe it.

It was late, so we stayed overnight in a hotel on the way. After all, it was still another four hours back to Wuppertal. Perhaps my parents wanted to let everything settle first. Maybe they, too, needed some time to take a step back and calmly digest my return.

The next morning, 12 July, I went down to the breakfast room and found that my father was already there. My mother was still in their room. While we were drinking our coffee at the table, he abruptly asked, 'Who actually gave you the right to do that to your mother?' It was the first and only question he asked. Well, who indeed had given me the right?

I looked at my father, my eyes wide, and answered, 'I did, who else?'

My father said nothing and remained silent the rest of the day, not wishing to know any further details about my time in prison, or about the trial, or what had motivated me to help people escape in the first place. The psychological impasse that prevented an exchange between us was palpable. But could I really blame him? Couldn't I have begun the dialogue?

As expected, my mother reacted quite differently, asking a lot of questions and repeating, 'To me, you're a hero. And the main thing is that you're healthy, my boy.'

We drove to Wuppertal-Barmen, where I spent the night at my parents' house on Wittelsbacherstrasse. My mother had lovingly made up my room, as always, and I slept where I had last lain about a year earlier, inexplicably ill in bed for days. The next morning at our second breakfast together, my father confronted me: 'In February 1962 you took your final school exams. It's now mid-1967, and you still don't have a university degree. If I remember correctly, we had agreed on seven semesters of law after you discontinued your engineering course in the autumn of 1963. Because of the special circumstances, I'll grant you an eighth semester.'

I looked intensely at my father: 'You expect me to finish the rest of my courses and take the exam in two semesters?'

'It won't be easy, but I'm sure you're extremely motivated to complete your studies, and your helping people to escape has proven to everyone that you have enormous energy.'

I was stupefied but had no good immediate response. He was not entirely wrong, and at that moment my pride kept me from pointing out the time I had served in prison. Nevertheless, his coldness hurt me. It had not even been thirty-six hours since we had met at the border, and this was the first thing he wanted to say to me. More than anything else it showed me how deeply aggrieved and disillusioned he was. In other words, I had 'done that' not only to my mother, but to him as well. Most of all to him. Following my temporary suspension from secondary school shortly before I was to take the final exams, my involvement as an escape helper and my subsequent imprisonment in Hohenschönhausen were the last straw.

After eight and a half semesters I took the first level of my state exams to qualify as a lawyer and passed with honours. I sent my father a copy of the certificate without a word.

My father died a few years later, in 1972. We had made our peace with each other not long before. During that time he showed me all the warmth that my behaviour had previously stifled in him. His more relaxed approach stemmed partly from the fact that I was about to take my second set of law exams, which greatly reassured him.

My mother had suffered intensely while I was in prison. I could tell from the lines of grief that marked her face. For a long time she kept spontaneously hugging me.

'Do you know that you were called up for military service during your time in Hohenschönhausen?' she asked me one day. 'Your deferral had expired.'

I looked at my mother in surprise. 'That means father had to go to the district recruiting office while I was in prison to explain that his son was unfortunately in investigative custody in the GDR?'

'Yes, exactly.'

Somehow my mother managed a little smile, as though she also found the whole story slightly amusing. I couldn't suppress a grin.

IT ISN'T ALWAYS ABOUT PEOPLE

I had guessed correctly: I no longer had a flat in Bonn. But it had been friends, not my parents, who had cleared out my place on Bachstrasse while I was in remand custody. I had to start all over again – with my relationships too. Not long after my release, Barbara broke up with me; she had heard about her Berlin 'rival'. I could have explained everything to Barbara and might have been able to win her back, but I was too proud to run after her. It wasn't worth it, I thought. A person who leaves so quickly without waiting for an explanation would not be able to understand what I had done. It felt to me like emotional condemnation in absentia. In retrospect, I must admit that I had wronged her, for I had never confided in her, and she must have been surprised and shocked. Today I regret that I made no effort to explain things to her.

I quickly found a small apartment. And very soon I met Claudia, who came from an eminent family of conservative politicians. Claudia and I had good times together. In May 1968, to the horror of her family, she and I marched at the front of a demonstration through Bonn to protest against the introduction of so-called emergency legislation. It was intended to amend West Germany's constitution to ensure the state's ability to act even in times of severe crisis, such as during wars or natural catastrophes. I saw it as state intervention in the fundamental rights of freedom, and therefore unacceptable.

Claudia was the first friend with whom I could speak about my imprisonment in Hohenschönhausen. Talk of escape help was largely avoided in the public sphere in order to protect the individuals concerned and to avoid jeopardising the difficult West German-East German negotiations on matters such as travel permits for West Berliners, the GDR transit agreement, the practice of buying people's freedom, and the reuniting of divided families.

Claudia asked many questions: 'What motivated you? What were you thinking? How did you cope with imprisonment?' The conversations with her opened me up. She wanted to know every detail, all the things in which my parents had shown little interest. At last I could breathe a sigh of relief. I felt from her the support I had lacked from my father – the reassurance that by helping people escape I had done something good.

* * *

For a long time I could not get my mind off the Stasi's attempt to recruit me. I did not want to burden Claudia with that, so I told Jürgen Stange about it.

'You must report it to the West German authorities immediately,' the West Berlin attorney advised urgently.

'But why? It was a transparent manoeuvre by intelligence agents. Why should the German judiciary be interested in it? Surely they don't care.'

Stange did not budge. 'Don't underestimate the German judiciary. It takes a hard line on relations with the GDR. You would do well to disclose the matter quickly. Take what you experienced there seriously.' He looked at me searchingly and then added, 'Or could you be in danger?'

'What do you mean?' I was perplexed.

'Volker, don't be naïve!'

'I still don't understand what you mean?'

The lawyer stared at me with increasing intensity until the penny finally dropped.

'They don't honestly think I want to become an agent?'

'Perhaps even a double agent. It has all happened before.'

I shook my head in amusement. Stange remained unmoved.

'Volker, if you don't report it, I'll have to, I'm afraid.'

'OK, I'll take care of it,' I muttered, somewhat subdued.

'That's good to hear.' Stange seemed satisfied.

A few weeks later – by that time it was summer – he rang me to follow up on our conversation. I had to tell him that I still I had not reported the matter.

'Oh, I'll do it when I have the time and the inclination. I have no reason to go to Berlin at the moment.'

'You can forget about time and inclination straight away. It's not just high time, it's highest!'

I had to address the political branch of the state prosecution services in Berlin and was directed to prosecutor Karl-Heinz Dobbert whose office was on Turmstrasse.

'Let's hear what you have to report,' Dobbert said after I had passed on greetings from Stange. Dobbert was in his mid-forties and had a pleasantly calm and matter-of-fact manner.

I told him about the visit I had received from the two Stasi officers in leather jackets the day before my release from the GDR, cited the address they had dictated to me, and explained: 'They wanted me to help put an end to Wolfgang Fuchs's activities.'

'We are aware of that,' Dobbert said. 'It's nothing new. They often try to draw western captives to their side. But thank you for informing us. We always want to know exactly what's going on over there in East Berlin.'

The time in Hohenschönhausen had other after effects as well. My lawyers in East and West Berlin wanted to be paid. The invoices arrived a few weeks after my release. Although both Stange and Vogel received handsome annual fees from the Federal Republic, Vogel charged me DM 1,500 (then around $375), not a small amount in those days. But I found it acceptable. Amazingly, however, I was to transfer the money to an account in West Berlin. Yes, he was admitted there as a lawyer, but, I assume, he also wanted to hedge some of his income in the west. I could imagine that a person in his delicate role could easily fall from grace. But he surely did not live only from these fees; he was on the Stasi payroll and was also paid by the Federal Republic, which perhaps explains the western bank account. He was receiving a good slice of the pie. As far as I could learn, he had little tax to pay on these fees in the GDR and was probably able to invest them profitably in the Federal Republic.

My father paid the bill for me; I did not have enough money in my account. I felt uncomfortable about that and tried to find a way to pay him back as quickly as possible. Our relationship was still strained, and I hoped this gesture might help relieve the situation somewhat. I therefore filed for support, basing my claim on the Prisoners' Aid Act (HHG), 'legislation on aid for persons who were taken into custody outside the Federal Republic of Germany for political reasons'. However, this source provided me with only modest sums, including DM 100 as 'welcome money'. That was not enough to cover Vogel's invoice. So I turned directly to the Ministry for All-German Affairs and, to my surprise, ultimately received full reimbursement. A large weight fell from my shoulders.

Unfortunately, the repayment did not help to improve the relationship between my father and me. He still asked no questions. The whole topic became strictly taboo. Today, in an incomparably more transparent society, such silence is hardly imaginable. But even when I visited my fraternity house in Heidelberg, no one asked me about what I had experienced. It seemed to me that the term 'escape help' had a bad reputation. The archives of the Stasi and the West German government were not yet accessible, and the escape helpers kept quiet. Nor were there yet any convincing, well-researched books on the subject. In other words, there was no persuasive way of coming to grips with the past.

* * *

I was diligent and disciplined in my studies, seeking to complete five courses and prepare for my exams, all in two semesters. I wanted to rise to my father's challenge. It required enormous effort. My father was visibly relieved. His ne'er-do-well son had finally become a man to be taken seriously.

As soon as I had a little more free time, I realised that the experience of imprisonment could not simply be shaken off like an annoying fly. I became increasingly aware that I had not been the only one arrested, and I began to take a closer interest in the fates of the other people involved. What had become of Kamal Hamdi? I found out that he had been escorted by a Stasi officer onto an Interflug plane from Berlin's Schönefeld airport to Damascus. A slight hitch, however, was that no direct flights existed between the two cities. During the stopover in Cyprus, Hamdi used a second passport sewn into his jacket and slipped away from his guard, transforming himself from escape helper to refugee. From Cyprus he travelled to the Federal Republic of Germany, where he received asylum in Bonn. Shortly thereafter, he was condemned to death in absentia by a military court in Damascus. Irrefutable proof of his complicity was contained in the report sent by the GDR government to then-president and general secretary of Syria's Baath Party – Hafiz al-Assad, the father of today's president of Syria. On 18 October 1967 the newspaper *Neues Deutschland*, the SED's main newspaper, carried an article headlined: 'Traitor sentenced in Syria':

> While serving as employees at the General Consulate of the S[yrian] A[rab] R[epublic] in the GDR, the convicted persons had engaged in treasonous relations with West German spy organisations and had abetted human trafficking... The Damascus press ... reports that the two defendants[5] were found guilty of their 'crimes against the revolutionary order in the SAR' and were sentenced to death for their collaboration with a foreign power.

Like his fat friend on the Kurfürstendamm, Hamdi started a career as a carpet dealer in Bonn.

---

5 The reference is to Kamal Hamdi and the vice consul, Mohamed Abdul Wali.

Joachim and Hannerose Meister, the couple who had been presented to me in the Magdalenenstrasse Stasi prison on the night of my arrest, were sentenced to four years in prison, of which they had to serve more than two and a half. At least they were released early. Stange told me about it, and three years after their release I went to see them in Nuremberg – the only escapees I felt the urge to meet up with and speak to again.

My older sister Lilo lived in Nuremberg, and when I visited her and her husband, I asked whether she would drive me to the Meisters' address. The couple was at home. They welcomed me into their living room.

'I'm very sorry for what happened,' I said over coffee and cake, 'we all had to pay a price for it.' The Meisters waved this aside.

'We're so glad that we didn't have to serve all four years.'

'What I'd really like to ask you is: could you hear anything going on outside the boot of the car?'

They both shook their heads. 'Not much. There was too much noise from the car and the streets. We could only hear a radio playing classical music. That helped calm us down a little.'

'Were you exchanged?'

'No,' said Joachim. 'We were bought out and driven by bus to Herleshausen with many others.' I was overwhelmed by a flood of memories, and my questions were jumbled. 'And what happened at Checkpoint Charlie when you were arrested?'

Mrs Meister spoke first. 'When the Mercedes stopped for a while, much longer than for a change of traffic lights, we knew that we'd reached the border. But the moment the boot of the car was opened and we saw the uniformed GDR officers, we realised what had happened.'

'And you were brought directly from Magdalenenstrasse to Hohenschönhausen?' Mr Meister nodded.

'So we were there at the same time,' I observed.

'Without knowing it,' Mrs Meister added.

This encounter was very important for me. We had shared an attempted escape, our arrest on the same day, and finally our release due to the efforts of both German states. Returning to my sister's home, I felt the visit had somehow closed this chapter of my life. Being an escape helper had finally been consigned to the past.

Living in Bonn rather than in Berlin, the capital of spies and escape helpers, I had not yet really reconnected with my old Berlin friends. Over time, my opinion of Wolfgang Fuchs also changed. I met him a few times after my release whenever I was in Berlin, but I gradually had to concede that we had no genuine bond of friendship. It was our common project that had connected us. He had bought an apartment building in Berlin-Neukölln, opened a pharmacy, and regularly surrounded himself with former escape helpers whose admiration he manifestly enjoyed. But I increasingly had the feeling that he was primarily interested in himself. His conspicuous lack of interest in the details of my imprisonment surprised and hurt me. After all, I had helped his second wife escape.

I especially remember an outing with him and a number of his friends on his boat, sailing along Wannsee, the large recreational lake in southwest Berlin. Naturally, I longed to ask Wolfgang what he had thought and done upon hearing of my arrest, but something held me back. I just silently watched the man who had somehow become a stranger to me. All at once I realised that I did not actually feel any connection to him, that we no longer had anything to say to each other, and that I no longer admired or even trusted him.

After returning to Bonn, I told Claudia about the boat trip with Wolfgang and his friends. She took me in her arms. She understood that it was difficult for me to acknowledge the change in my perception of Fuchs, my realisation that I, too, had ultimately just been part of his 'business'. To some extent I was disappointed that he and his friends had discussed the 'role of money' in escape aid during our boat trip.

Claudia pushed me back with both arms to look directly into my eyes. 'And then you suddenly knew that Wolfgang was not simply a good, selfless human being.' I nodded.

'Did you never think about how he financed your trips? What about the diplomats?' Claudia smiled. 'A boat like that on Wannsee and a pharmacy don't appear out of nowhere.'

'Actually, I was OK with the idea that he took money; he did have a family to feed. But the thought that he might have earned so much that he was able to invest in property never occurred to me.'

Like many people who unexpectedly come into so much money, Fuchs lost it quickly. In 1976 he started converting Cadillacs into escape cars. He bought his first luxury American car from Hasso Herschel. Other cars followed with which he organised escapes from Czechoslovakia and Hungary to Bavaria, sometimes to Austria. His businesses went badly. He told me that some of his assets were embezzled by a 'friend'. He enjoyed little support and happiness from his family. He ended up spending the colder half of the year in India, living extremely frugally. Impoverished, ill, and forlorn, he died in 2001 at the age of 62. I said my final farewell to him at his funeral.

Apart from studying, I delved into Marxist literature, reading *Das Kapital* – one of the ways of coming to grips with my time in Hohenschönhausen. I regarded my episode as an escape helper as something I had put behind me. It no longer moved or interested me to see and hear the old escape helper stories in ever-changing guises.

In fact, perhaps the escape helpers and I were more a kind of temporary community, sharing a common fate and a common interest. But it was not the community that I had imagined it to be. I was more sobered than disillusioned. I did maintain contact with Jürgen, Ulrich, and Manfred, but two of them lived in other cities. They had been escape helpers within a group. I had been more of a lone wolf.

SLUSH FUNDS – AND MILITARY OVERCOATS ON THE TRANSIT ROUTE

Hadn't I acquired the basics of Russian during my detention? What was the use of all that effort if it couldn't be used? Despite my experience in prison, my thirst for adventure continued unabated. But I quenched it with somewhat less audacious undertakings. In 1971 I applied to a Berlin tour company to work for a year as a tour guide in Moscow. I did not mention that I had never been to the Russian capital. The tour company was delighted, given that Russian language skills were not exactly in plentiful supply in the West in the early seventies.

And so I flew to Moscow. On Red Square I bought a newspaper and announced to my group: 'We're standing here on Red Square, which is almost octagonal, and we're surrounded by impressive architecture. To the east, for example, you see the beautiful St. Basil's Cathedral and the Lenin mausoleum, with the Kremlin wall running from the northwest to the southeast, and to the northeast you see the department store GUM...' Although all my knowledge for the tours was drawn from books, I seemed to come across convincingly.

What mattered most was how incredibly satisfying it felt to have passable reading skills in Russian and the ability to hold basic conversations with Muscovites. The time in Hohenschönhausen had not been completely wasted. At least it had given me skills in another language. Filled with pride, I showed the travel group the many sights as though I had personally created them.

* * *

After a number of trips to Moscow, the serious side of life awaited me. I worked in Munich as a German articled clerk and then moved on to the municipal court in Garmisch-Partenkirchen, a few months later to the regional court in Traunstein, and finally to the higher regional court in the northern German city of Schleswig.

I followed Jürgen Stange's career for some time and temporarily worked as an articled clerk in his law office after passing my first state examination in law. Stange later offered me a partnership. I thanked him for his offer but declined. He was still primarily involved in buying people's freedom, and for obvious reasons I was not suited for that work. It would certainly have appealed to me, but for the GDR I was clearly a spent force. My career as a political lawyer would have ended before it had ever even begun.

Like Vogel, Stange had seized the opportunity that lay in buying the freedom of GDR prisoners. I do not know how the two men met, but they developed an historically unique, quasi-monopolistic business model for legal work. Vogel proved to be the financially cleverer of the two. He survived the unification of Germany almost unscathed in terms of both criminal prosecution and material wealth, whereas Stange quietly descended into poverty, losing his licence to practice law and to serve as a notary.

Unlike Vogel, Stange was an outgoing man of great charm, which he directed particularly towards women. He later became entangled in the so-called Hirt scandal. Edgar Hirt was an assistant secretary of state under Federal Minister Egon Franke and succeeded Herbert Wehner in the Ministry for All-German Affairs. It was this ministry from which DM 5.6 million (about $2.69 million) were said to have disappeared without a trace between 1979 and 1982. At the time, it was claimed that the millions of Deutsche Mark had been deliberately manoeuvred past the controllers of West Germany's lower house of parliament, the Bundestag, ostensibly for sensitive operations conducted to buy the freedom of prisoners in the East. Every additional person with this knowledge would have been one too many. According to newspaper reports, in 1978 Franke and Hirt had come up with the idea of creating slush funds. Until then, the resources for the 'federal government's special efforts' had been covered in section 27, chapter 02 of the budget. However, both men considered that politically awkward, in particular for secretive operations. As they later argued, they needed a free hand without having to defer to uninformed inquisitive controllers.

It was Stange who actually introduced the slush funds to the two major churches in Germany. He approached Heinz-Dietrich Thiel, the West Berlin Director of Caritas, the Catholic relief organisation, and suggested that a reserve fund be created for humanitarian purposes. According to the magazine *Spiegel* (March 1984), the method was simple:

> Caritas was to receive federal grants for the delivery of medical equipment to the GDR and then siphon off part of the money for special payments involving clandestine East-West transactions.

Stange later insisted that Franke and Hirt had knowledge of this. Thiel sought the counsel and agreement of ranking church representatives, such as East Berlin's Cardinal Alfred Bengsch... From 1979 to 1982, Caritas received approximately 10.9 million marks of government funding; about 5.6 million marks went back to the ministry. In 27 cases, the devout helpers forked out between 10,000 and 700,000 marks. The cash was usually delivered by Stange, who acted as the go-between with the Ministry of All-German Affairs.

In 1986 Jürgen Stange was charged with aiding and abetting the misappropriation of funds, but ultimately not tried. However, Minister Egon Franke and ministerial director Edgar Hirt were both convicted.

* * *

I gradually came to understand that the churches were conduits for such economic deals. The first transportation of cash to free prisoners is said to have taken place in Berlin at Lehrter Stadtbahnhof (today's Central Railway Station) with the cash hidden in an inner pocket of Stange's jacket. Buying freedom was still in its Wild West phase. But the government wanted to solve the budgetary technicalities by keeping them more in line with budget regulations, resulting in the route via the churches. Many East German citizens were Protestant, in particular Lutheran, and their church was known throughout Germany as the 'Evangelical Church of Germany' (Evangelische Kirche in Deutschland, or EKD). A German-wide institution, its representatives were not restricted by political boundaries, even after the Federal Republic of Germany and the German Democratic Republic had been founded in 1949. The Lutheran churches in West and East Germany had common church representatives, including a joint diocese of Berlin.

The western churches helped build a society rooted in democracy and solidarity, particularly in the 1950s, and they very quickly began to send care packages containing gifts to the GDR. Financial aid was more difficult to manage. West and East Germany did not recognise each other as states, and transferring money was prohibited. Cash had to be brought over the border illegally in suitcases, an act that was criminally prosecuted with such determination by the GDR that it was soon no longer an option.

In the severe winter of 1956, the GDR needed coal for heating. Nevertheless, the Polish head of state, Władysław Gomułka, in need of coal for his own country, halted the supply to the GDR, which had no hard currency with which to buy coal on the world market. The coal was urgently needed to keep the GDR's power plants running. The situation led the GDR to initiate 'Church Deal A' through the EKD in West Germany. Under this arrangement, 60,000 tons of coal were bought with West German money in the United States and delivered to the GDR, with the East German government paying the price in GDR marks to the East German regional churches. The Federal Republic permitted this unofficial trade only 'with the greatest reservations' and on the condition that it would be the only such transaction. However, the success of the operation made both sides see their own advantages in any future cooperation: The GDR received hard currency or the equivalent material support, and the FRG was able to help their East German compatriots with supply of energy. Similar types of deals amounting to 40 or 50 million Deutsche Mark annually were henceforth struck through the churches.

Buying the release of prisoners became the basis for developing 'Church Deal B'. Deals conducted with the Catholic Church were labelled with a 'C'. As of 1966, the East German authority responsible for this process was the 'Commercial Coordination' (KoKo) section in the Ministry of Foreign Trade, headed by Alexander Schalck-Golodkowski. Mielke's confidant Colonel Volpert was the supervising Stasi officer of both Vogel and Schalck-Golodkowski – the former organising the flow of hard currency to the GDR, the latter spending part of it by founding, or buying, profitable companies in West Germany.

Many years later, Vogel told me that I had been exchanged for two spies and probably also for money. It had not been by chance that he and Stange had needed to take care of 'business' at the Herleshausen border crossing. Vogel was unable to say anything more to me about it though, and probably was not allowed to, which led me to think that the EKD archive might contain documents pertaining to me. Of course, I was keenly interested to know how much money had been involved in my case. I called the archive and asked to speak with one of their archivists.

'Good morning, my name is Volker Heinz,' I explained. 'I served time in Hohenschönhausen in pre-trial custody and would like to have an appointment to examine what you have about me in your archive.'

The archivist on the other end of the line cleared his throat and said, 'Before you set out, we should first look to see if we have anything relating to you at all. I'll call you back as soon as I have any information.' He kept his promise. Two or three days later, he rang to inform me of the results of his search.

'Mr Heinz, I have in fact found your name.'

'Good, then I can come over to see you.'

'You needn't bother. There are only a few documents, and I can post copies to you.'

I was suddenly very excited. The matter was clear to me. If the EKD archive had anything about me at all, then it could only mean that money had indeed been involved in my release. That made sense to me. Why should the GDR have relinquished the chance to extract payment for me if money was paid for every East German citizen wanting to emigrate? The archivist summarised the result of his efforts in a brief letter, but made no reference to specific sums.

Dear Mr Heinz,

It is correct that you are mentioned in connection with the Clemens case (File EZA 742/294):

On 9th May, Countess von Rittberg informed Assistant Secretary Rehlinger about the pending pardon of Clemens. 'Minister Heinemann has no doubt that the federal president will most likely approve the request. On the other hand, he thinks that one should at least try to use the case for an exchange.' Rehlinger replied on 10th May: 'The way things stand at the moment, I would like to recommend that everything be attempted to defer a decision for another three weeks if at all possible. A response to our offer is certain to arrive in the coming days... Aside from that, I already have a specific matter in mind. It concerns Volker Heinz; the case is certainly known to you. Perhaps we should discuss the issue again after Whitsun.'

I made further inquiries regarding the amount of money involved in the federal archive in Koblenz. But to this day my own files are under seal. My name appears only in individual documents and written notes by Hanns Martin Schleyer, the federal government, and my attorneys Vogel and Stange.

Regaining my freedom was wonderful, but the road to my release was anything but typical. It helped a lot that I neither asked for nor received money. But more important was the protection afforded by Schleyer and Knieper, the skilful negotiations by my lawyers, and their good relations with their respective governments. My case was atypical for another reason: an escape helper was exchanged for two spies – KGB spies at that! – in addition to the extra payment. The price for my freedom was high, for the West German government, but also for me.

* * *

On 27 June 1972 my probation period[6] ended. Just two days later I was sitting in my car, driving from Heidelberg to Berlin. It was the first time since my arrest that I was crossing the border into East Germany at Helmstedt. Alert and tense, I nervously gripped the steering wheel. I felt insecure, imagining that Stasi officers and East German soldiers might suddenly appear to arrest and detain me again. But nothing of the sort happened, and when I reached West Berlin, I shouted for joy. I'd made it. I could move freely again. No traps had ensnared me.

The following winter I moved back to Berlin, the city of my destiny, both now and then. I decided to drive to Prague

---

6 East German Head of State Walter Ulbricht had commuted six years of my sentence, the limit under the East German criminal code. In addition to the nearly one year I had already served by the time of my trial, his act had left five years of my sentence to be served on probation after my release from prison.

to visit friends I had not seen for years. Again, there were no complications either at the frontier or along the way. The return trip, however, was quite another thing. It was a bitterly cold day, snow lay on the streets. I used the Cínovec–Zinnwald border crossing, the highest point in the eastern Erzgebirge, about 28 miles (45 kilometres) from Dresden. A snowstorm had started, and a heavy wind whipped flurries of snowflakes through the wintery forests. The Czech officials only glanced at my ID, then I approached the hut of the East German border guard. I rolled down the window to present my papers. The very moment I passed them to the guard, a gust of wind tore the documents from my hand. He ran after them, and I jumped out of the car to help track them down. Groping for the vital papers on the other side of the lane, we fell over each other in the snow. That was the first shock of the night.

We struggled to our feet and quickly returned to the car, mutually excusing ourselves for our clumsiness. The guard examined my passport and finally waved me through. It took me almost an hour to reach Dresden. The snowfall was so heavy that I could travel only at about 30 miles (50 kilometres) an hour. The windscreen wipers barely managed to push the white masses of snow aside.

From Dresden, the transit autobahn continued towards Dreilinden in Berlin's southwest. This stretch (from Dresden to Berlin) was the only permitted route for a West German. But even on this road it was impossible to travel at a higher speed, because, quite apart from the havoc wreaked by the snow, the surface was in very poor condition.

While I battled on through the wintery chaos, I suddenly noticed two men standing on the side of the road flagging me down. They were wearing military overcoats. I struggled to keep calm. What did they want? The car heating was on the highest setting, but I suddenly broke out in a cold sweat. I pulled over to the edge of the road. The men in their heavy overcoats approached me. What in heaven's name were they after? I rolled down my window, bracing myself for just about anything. To my astonishment, one of them asked whether I could perhaps help them, his teeth chattering violently from the cold. They must have been standing there for some time.

'Help? How can I help you?' Their request certainly surprised me. I had expected a lecture, an inspection, or even a reproach, although I was not aware of having committed any offence. But a request?

'We're stranded,' said the second man. 'We're stationed in Cottbus. We wanted to have a night out in Dresden, but our car has broken down. We haven't been able to fix it. We're outside our military district without permission and have to be back before midnight at the latest.'

'Otherwise you'll be punished?' I knew there were travel restrictions within the GDR, and they applied not only to the general public, but also, and especially, to soldiers.

'Exactly,' they replied in unison. 'Do you think you can tow us?'

That was forbidden! A criminal offence – making contact with the class enemy without permission, suspicion of military espionage. But my probation period had ended. Should I take the risk? What if we are caught? The whole thing all over again?

I can't explain why, but my empathy outweighed my reason: I decided to help them. I took the rope from my car and tied the two vehicles together. The man whose teeth had been chattering the most climbed into the driver's seat to steer the car; the other sat down on the back seat of my car to keep an eye on whether the rope was holding out.

The speed of the journey now slowed down to less than 20 miles an hour. My passenger said little, only that military service was pretty joyless, whilst I was totally preoccupied with steering our little all-German convoy safely through the snow. After about three quarters of an hour, we had made it. We had reached the exit at Guben, the military district in which the two soldiers were stationed. It was ten minutes to midnight.

'Gentlemen,' I said, 'unfortunately, I have to drop you off here. As you know, I'm not allowed to leave the transit autobahn. I expect and trust that you won't report our little adventure. I hope I've been able to help you a little. You'll probably have to complete the rest of your journey on foot. Best of luck with the rest of your journey.' With these words I uncoupled the two cars. They thanked me profusely as I quickly stowed the rope, and set off again.

Yet another experience I can't tell anyone about, I thought to myself. Good grief, Volker, when will you ever get over your helper's syndrome? Your family, your friends, not to mention Vogel and Stange, will think you're completely mad! I finally arrived at the Drewitz–Dreilinden checkpoint – also known as Checkpoint Bravo – just outside south-western Berlin. The border facilities were roofed over and very brightly lit. I waited in a queue of ten or fifteen cars being methodically checked. I had my papers ready, including my transit visa, which I had to present. Suddenly I glanced in the rear-view mirror and froze. On the back seat lay a soldier's cap that my passenger must have had left behind when leaving my car. All I could think was, 'Will this never end?'

I desperately tried to find a solution. I estimated that I had about ten minutes before it was my turn in the queue. Where could I hide the cap so that it wouldn't be noticed? I couldn't exactly just chuck it out of the window, so I tried to crumple it up as much as possible. The material was pretty stiff, and the plastic rim at the front complicated matters. When I had reduced the cap to as small a sphere as possible ('destruction of state property'!), I stuck it under the front seat and shoved part of the foot mat over it for good measure.

This time, though, luck was on my side. The border guards let me through. A single look into the car's interior satisfied them. I was not among those selected for a thorough search. As soon as I hit the open road again, shortly before entering West Berlin, I tossed the cap out of the window. Greetings to Guben and Cottbus!

Later, I told Jürgen Stange the story in his spacious office on Bundesallee. He turned white. 'Tell me, Volker, have you completely lost your senses? What are you doing towing GDR military personnel along the East German autobahn?'

I could not offer much in my defence, so I tried to explain by saying, 'Have you forgotten? I'm just a guy who likes to help.'

At least he found the response moderately funny. And it was a good reason to open his invariably well-stocked schnapps cabinet. We washed down the story with a generous drink.

MOABIT

Wolfgang Vogel was in prison. I read it in the *Spiegel* magazine in London. It was 1990, 23 years after my release, one year after the fall of the Wall. Wolfgang Vogel was 65 years old.

Vogel of all people. The man who had helped secure my release now himself had to experience what it meant to spend day after day in a prison cell. The bitter irony of fate. I would gladly have defended him myself, but his team of defence lawyers was already complete. Besides, I was working as a lawyer in London at the time. But the old bond to him kindled in me a great need to show him my solidarity. I spontaneously decided to visit Vogel in prison and took the next plane to Berlin. But how to arrange for permission to see him?

What was the background of the case against Vogel? All clients who had come to his East Berlin office seeking to emigrate to West Germany first had to answer a large number of questions. Among other things, they were obliged to fill out an application form disclosing the details about property they owned in the GDR. Whoever wanted to leave the GDR could not count on receiving permission to emigrate until their property had been transferred to a third party, usually to someone working for the Stasi. As Vogel was both a solicitor and a notary public, he could notarise the required deeds of sale, thereby transferring the property to a buyer at a very low price. After Germany's unification, real-estate prices in eastern Germany started to rise considerably. Some of Vogel's former clients claimed that he had taken advantage of them. In his defence, Vogel stated that the conditions were not his but rather those of his state. There was no question that he had notarised the contracts, but the clients could have gone to a different notary.

Because he travelled frequently, Vogel always had his staff prepare notarial documents before signing them. In one civil case for which Vogel had been summoned to appear as a witness, it emerged that he had not been present at the notarisation. Nevertheless, he had stated under oath that the notary's signature was his. The public prosecutor who had been pursuing Vogel and who knew of course that a notary was obliged to notarise his documents personally, established that Wolfgang Vogel had been in Israel at that time. As a result, Vogel was put in pre-trial custody in Berlin-Moabit for perjury and various other charges.

I knew one of Vogel's defence lawyers, the former wife of an escape helper from Fuchs's group.

'Can't you give me a delegated power of attorney, Charlotte?' I begged her in her Berlin law practice. I had come from London especially for this purpose and did not want to fly back without having seen Vogel.

'Don't you find that risky?' she asked.

'It's not illegal,' I replied.

'And why is it so important to you?'

'I'm appalled about his arrest. So is our government. But it can't get involved. The fraud charges against Vogel simply don't seem tenable,' I explained, as yet unaware of the perjury involved.

'It's not only about real estate, Volker. There are also charges of unjust enrichment and perjury.' I persisted.

'I'm sure he gave the false testimony in a moral dilemma – trying to save both his skin and the purchasers who otherwise would have lost their property. Of course he regrets it today. But I'm not concerned with the legal subtleties; I just want to show him my solidarity.'

'And now you find it terrible that his pristine image is being stained?'

'Nonsense, it probably never was pristine. His role was to manage a dreadful balancing act between two systems. He couldn't have come out of it unscathed. But I primarily want to thank him again. I would like to encourage him to look ahead. If I do something, I do it all the way. That's just the way I am.'

Charlotte sighed. She signed the required delegated power of attorney. I set out for the remand prison in Berlin-Moabit that very day. When Wolfgang Vogel was led into the visitors' room and saw me, tears welled up in his eyes. I couldn't suppress mine either. All the old memories suddenly overwhelmed me in a surge of emotion. My own time in prison painfully came alive again. The meetings with Vogel on Magdalenenstrasse. They were the only glimmer of hope I had. Now our situations were reversed. The outrage I felt about his imprisonment in light of the great services he had rendered was enormous. I was also angered by the public prosecutor's shamelessness in forcing Vogel's detention by asserting a perceived risk that Vogel would abscond. Vogel was an all-German figure in the truest sense of the term. He would never flee his country. Knowing from my own experience how helpless a person feels under such circumstances, I wanted to give Vogel a bit of hope.

'I am so sorry that we have to meet again under these sad circumstances,' I said at last, after trying to regain my composure. I found it hard to believe that he had instantly recognised me after so many years. He waved my words aside, still struggling with his tears.

'I really don't know what to say.'

I tried to console him, but clearly it was not easy. 'Wolfgang' – we used the familiar form of address, for we had become friends after my release – 'it's not so bad. I personally believe strongly in your innocence. Remember my case. Ultimately, everything was resolved.'

He smiled faintly. 'But it was much easier then than it is now. In those days all that mattered was a political solution. If I had the consent from Honecker, Mielke, or Streit, the handover went ahead. The courts had nothing to say. Due process is indeed a bit more complicated than that.'

'Yes, I know.' I felt helpless, not knowing quite how to express my gratitude again or what specific help I could offer him. I hadn't thought about it much beforehand. I had simply wanted to see him. Vogel insinuated something that further upset me: 'I won't emerge from this unscathed.' I tried again to lift his spirits.

'When you're in custody, the world looks a lot gloomier than it really is. After your long experience with inmates, you know that yourself better than anyone. Given the 30,000 prisoners you helped free, I can't imagine that the Federal Court of Justice will send you to jail.'

'Well, I do at least have a little political backing,' Vogel noted with a timid smile.

'How so?' I asked urgently.

'Former Chancellor Helmut Schmidt has visited me. So has Jürgen Schmude, the former federal minister of justice.'

He said nothing more about the meetings with the two politicians. Discretion had always been his trade secret, and it was no different now. I had once asked him directly who the two spies had been for whom I had been exchanged and how much money had been involved in my release. He did not answer either question. 'I hope you'll understand that,' he had added.

Of course I understood. In the final analysis, it was not his personal secret. It was the secret of the West German and East German governments. How gladly I would have worked for Wolfgang Vogel in matters of buying the freedom of prisoners. I found his profession immensely fascinating.

When I left the prison that day, I was still in turmoil. My detention had left deep scars. Even though decades had passed since then, there were times when everything resurfaced. Wolfgang Vogel had been a symbol of hope to me at that time. His few words had helped me bear a great deal. Yes, it was immense gratitude that I felt towards him.

I walked through Moabit, pondering. There was a little time left until my return flight. I couldn't get Vogel out of my mind. He was a much admired master of crossing borders and boundaries and had to walk many a tightrope, both politically and personally. One example was the separation from his first wife. After the Wall went up, she had urged him to leave the GDR. That was out of the question for Wolfgang. In 1966 the couple divorced and his former wife moved to West Germany and Austria with their two children (Vogel had secured her new citizenship). I suspect he had to pay a heavy price for that, which certainly would have included loyalty to the party line. Not long thereafter, he met a young woman from Essen, Helga Fritsch, who became his secretary and wife. Astonishingly, the communist state accepted his relationship with a woman from the West – an indication of how important, even outright indispensable Vogel was in the buying out of political prisoners. There was, of course, the GDR's insatiable hunger for hard currency. Just as Germany's unification later fell to Helmut Kohl in 1990, Vogel, who worked in a geopolitical situation dominated by the Cold War, grabbed this unique professional opportunity with both hands.

I once asked Vogel, 'Wolfgang, did you ever have the desire to leave the GDR for good?'

'Sure,' he said, 'I played with the idea occasionally.'

'Then why didn't you?'

'They would undoubtedly have killed me. Traitors were ruthlessly eliminated. Besides, what would have become of my clients? At the very least, there would have been long delays until the delicate network of lawyers in East and West would have been re-established.'

Vogel was sentenced to one year in prison. Since he had already served about the same time in investigative custody, his sentence was shortened and he was released early. For a lawyer, being convicted of perjury was a terrible blow, and a very bitter one. The public prosecutor who had wanted to make a name for himself with Vogel's case suffered complete defeat over the other charges. The appeal to the Federal Court of Justice failed as well. Wolfgang was a free man, but he was forced to renounce his licence to practice law, not unlike Jürgen Stange after his arraignment and ensuing loss of reputation and income.

Vogel was indeed an enigmatic character. On the one hand he was the solicitous servant of a partially criminal system; on the other hand he helped many people gain their freedom by virtue of his enormous negotiating skills, great discretion, and his dogged perseverance. He was a devout Catholic. His success filled him with immense joy and deep satisfaction. I can well imagine how he must have felt as he sat across from my parents and could report to them: 'We'll be getting your son out very soon.' Grateful eyes must have met his.

Recalling his encounters with Vogel, former German Federal Chancellor Helmut Schmidt aptly described the lawyer's act of straddling two systems by forging a Faustian pact with the Stasi: 'It was a feat ... to win the trust of West Germans yet not lose the trust of the Communists... To me, he came across as a reliable human being. The human dimension was the deciding factor.' Vogel had prepared Schmidt's 1981 trip to the GDR. When Vogel died in 2008, Schmidt wrote in his obituary: 'We all owe him gratitude and respect.' I whole-heartedly share that sentiment.

I have often asked myself where a person like Vogel drew his strength from. I think the answer lies in his faith. The Catholic Church is redemptive: it affords the possibility to confide one's inner conflicts to a representative of the Almighty through confession. The Catholic Church forgives a great deal. It enabled Vogel to bear everything. To me, the faith of this discreet East German lawyer was the key to comprehending him. It was also the reason for his healthy, level-headed pragmatism. Lawyers, not unlike doctors, earn from the misfortunes of others. But Vogel's legacy reached beyond the financial aspects of his profession – far beyond.

EPILOGUE

Friday 9 September 2016 marked fifty years since the day of my arrest, a good occasion for further reflections.

After my release from prison, I set about personally thanking everyone who had contributed to reducing my detention so dramatically: Wolfgang Vogel, Jürgen Stange, and, in recognition of the West German government's role, the Federal Minister of Intra-German Relations.

I also expressed my deep appreciation to my fraternity brothers Werner Knieper and Hanns Martin Schleyer, whose intercession had paved the way to setting me free. Despite, or perhaps precisely because of the gratitude I felt, particularly to Schleyer, I left Suevia in the 1970s without giving any official reason. I left because I no longer wished to belong to a fraternity whose members did not publicly discuss and come to grips with its National Socialist past, indeed a fraternity that even actively sought to conceal it.

In 1966 I was unaware of the part Schleyer had played in such Nazi enanglements. But despite the fraternity's internal taboo on disclosure, I gradually learned of details that did not become more widely known until September 1977, when the newspapers and television stations released a shocking photograph of Schleyer, who had since become the president of both the German Employers' Association and the Federal Association of German Industries. He was shown seated in an undershirt and an unzipped training jersey beneath the logo of the Red Army Faction, the German urban terrorist group that had kidnapped him. Overnight, Schleyer became one of the most famous citizens of the Federal Republic, with journalists unearthing one detail after another. His Nazi past and his powerful positions had motivated the Red Army Faction to abduct him and hold him hostage in an attempt to force the West German government to release other terrorist prisoners.

Because Schleyer had gone to such lengths to achieve my release, I could not have confronted him at the time. Yet I found myself in a moral dilemma that demanded resolution. I saw no other way than quietly leaving the fraternity.

Many of my fraternity brothers considered this decision outrageous and deeply ungrateful. I kept silent but maintained contact to my closer friends, including Schleyer's eldest son. Many years later I returned to Suevia at the request of my fraternity brothers, determined to write the fraternity's history during the Third Reich. In 2010, having meanwhile been elected the fraternity's chairman, I wrote an essay entitled 'Suevia under the Third Reich'. It was part of the fraternity's commemorative volume published on the occasion of the 200th anniversary of our founding. I am sure that Schleyer – a courageous, but above all honest man – would have welcomed my article (the text of which his eldest son had approved in advance).

The limits of tolerance among my fraternity brothers became evident, however, when I urged the fraternity to apologise personally and publicly to the descendants of our Jewish fraternity brothers who had been banned by our fraternity under government pressure in 1935, and to have an independent committee of historians produce a brochure reappraising the fraternity's past. I could not win majority approval for this project. To avoid a rift, I resigned as chairman. Here again, I am convinced that Schleyer would have gone along with my idea of facing up to the past.

The fact that both German states accepted the principle of recognising the criminal convictions of their respective citizens meant that my East German sentence had to be recorded in West Germany's Central Criminal Register. Preventing this required a decision by the Public Prosecutor's Office in West Germany, a step for which I had petitioned soon after my release. Because of the obviously political nature of my conviction, the decision not to register my conviction was taken without much debate. The GDR verdict itself was rescinded in 1992 by the Berlin regional court's ruling, accepting the application I had filed after unification. In the meantime the East German verdict survived in purely formal terms for about twenty-five years, but it never hampered me either professionally or privately.

My attitude towards the GDR was never marked by hatred. Scepticism, criticism, and rejection – yes, of course. But hatred? No. Nevertheless, my overall assessment took form relatively early: A state that treats its citizens in a manner that makes hundreds of thousands of them, even millions, want to flee, had to be dysfunctional. No complex historical scrutiny was needed to come to this conclusion. All one had to do was watch East

German television's propaganda programme *Der schwarze Kanal* (The Black Channel), in which journalist Karl-Eduard von Schnitzler took excerpts from western television and distorted them with commentary based on GDR ideology. A few episodes would probably have sufficed to motivate me to help people in the GDR – had I not already been motivated anyway.

Forty-six years after my activities as a young escape helper, German Federal President Joachim Gauck wanted to honour me for that commitment. I was to receive the Order of Merit on Ribbon of the Federal Republic of Germany (*Bundesverdienstkreuz am Band*) on 29 August, 2012.

I made my way to the Berlin regional office of the State of Hesse. I liked the address: 5 Ministergärten (Ministers' Gardens). A striking building of glass and sandstone, the grounds include a small slope lined with grapevines, mainly Riesling and Pinot noir, a little nod to the vineyards along Bergstrasse in the federal state of Hesse. Before the ceremony began, I saw Joachim Schreiber whom I had invited to attend.

'All I can say is congratulations,' he greeted me. 'But you know, we find it rather surprising that you are the only one receiving this medal.'

'Why?' I asked, somewhat puzzled. Standing around us were several other people, including my wife Sandra, who raised her eyebrows a little.

'Well, there are others who can take similar credit.'

Did Joachim feel they had been overlooked? 'Manfred has already received the Order of Merit of the Federal Republic of Germany,' I responded. 'To my knowledge, he was the first escape helper to be honoured. Such decisions probably take a fairly long time to reach. Besides, my acceptance speech will make it clear that I am receiving this medal on behalf of all those escape helpers who likewise sacrificed a great deal to be involved.'

Manfred Baum had received the same award two years earlier. After he had continued his studies at Heidelberg University, he completed his doctorate in Hamburg, where he worked for many years as an oncologist. He died about a year after I was honoured. At about the same time, a large group of escape helpers (among them, to my astonishment, a few 'commercially oriented' ones) received awards similar to mine. I was happy to see Joachim Schreiber and Ulrich Bahnsen acknowledged in this way.

The ceremony began. The medal was conferred on me for 'enormous civic courage and desire for freedom'. I expressed my thanks, calling to mind my friend Manfred Baum through whom I had originally joined the group of escape helpers: Ulrich Bahnsen, Joachim Schreiber, and Wolfgang Fuchs. It was especially important to me to mention Reinhard Furrer, later to become West Germany's legendary first astronaut, who had driven me to the checkpoint at Heinrich Heine Strasse on the day of my arrest. I also expressed my heartfelt thanks and gratitude to my fraternity brothers Hanns Martin Schleyer and Manfred Knieper. Had Schleyer not pressed my case in Bonn, I do not know whether I would have had to serve all or most of my sentence. To me, the most important passage of my acceptance speech was this:

Those of us who aided and abetted escapes in the early years of the Wall regarded ourselves as humanitarian helpers without ever thinking of thanks, praise, or even remuneration. I do not remember the word *hero* having ever being used. These activities, distracting me from my studies, were rather suspect to my father as he clearly indicated when he and my mother picked me up at the border near Herleshausen after my release. Only in the eyes of my fiercely loyal and proud mother did I gain respect.

As I lay in bed that night, I thought back to the time when the Wall fell, suddenly doing away with the need for tunnels, converted vehicles, fake passports and bribed diplomats. I was in London at the time. The news overwhelmed me so much that I sat in front of the television and cried like a little boy. I had served time in the GDR because of that Wall, and its demise was to me a highly personal symbol of freedom. I could not really share my emotional response with my fellow lawyers and friends. Many people in Britain remained as sceptical as their prime minister, Margaret Thatcher, and her counterpart in France, President François Mitterand. Only the Americans under George H. W. Bush and the citizens of the Soviet Union under Mikhail Gorbachev, after initial hesitation, committed themselves to Germany's unification.

Almost naïvely, Chancellor Kohl dramatically overestimated the short- and medium-term economic prospects of the former GDR's economy and its citizens. He spoke of flourishing landscapes, whereas others feared enormous strains on the old Federal Republic. But Kohl had instinctively found the right tone for the people of the former GDR, who were apprehensive about ultimately being second-class citizens again if two independent German states were to emerge.

But what an achievement of the Federal Republic! After the Second World War, the country succeeded in integrating 14 million refugees from the eastern territories it had lost, followed by more from eastern Europe. After the fall of the

Wall, the FRG took 16 million GDR citizens economically under their wing, dismantled the existing East German economic structures and their ideological superstructure, and totally rebuilt them. Monumental effort was required in both western and eastern Germany. And today the refugees from the Middle East, Afghanistan, and Africa? How many million will there be? Three, four, five? Immense economic and cultural challenges await unified Germany, but they also offer opportunities to make amends for the wrongs that Germany committed against the world and millions of its own citizens under National Socialism.

In the late summer of 1992, I returned to Berlin after five years in London. I had qualified as an English barrister-at-law after two and a half years at university and law school. I then worked with an American law firm. During my frequent business trips from England to Germany, I repeatedly saw what remained of the fallen, crumbling wall. My city of destiny magically drew me back. After returning, I opened my first law office on Schiffbauerdamm, not far from the Friedrichstrasse S-Bahn station in former East Berlin, the place at which my excursions to the eastern part of Berlin had begun so many years earlier.

Not long afterwards, in 1994, I went to Hohenschönhausen for the first time after my imprisonment there. It had not been possible to visit the former prison much earlier. It had first continued as a prison and was then turned into a national memorial. As I entered the grounds of this once forbidden part of East Berlin, I did not cry, but I did wrestle with my memories and emotions. I had suspected that the site would move me. But I had not expected the experience to affect me as deeply as it did. The sight of the cells and the many interrogation rooms really got under my skin. For a long time I had thought of my detention at Hohenschönhausen of just under one year as only a marginal episode in my life. But returning to my former prison proved me emotionally wrong. Accompanied by my wife and children, I went to the 'recreation cage', in which I had fortified myself physically and mentally with push-ups during the prisoners' daily exercise sessions. I stood there in silence, looking up at the sky punctuated by barbed wire. The clouds floated by, and all my thoughts went with them. At that moment I felt infinitely free.

Finally, we went to the prison hospital in which Erich Mielke, former head of the Ministry of State Security (Stasi), had lain in 1990. In late 1989 he was charged with 'damaging the national economy' and murdering a policeman in the 1930s. Hohenschönhausen had been Mielke's Stasi prison, but in the end he himself became a prisoner there, caught in his own trap. What tragic symbolism.

Assisting escapes on humanitarian grounds has become a burning issue once again. In 2015 there was heated debate about whether German vacationers should be allowed to take refugees back to Germany with them in their cars, a violation of European Union border laws. It was not an easy matter to grapple with, just as when Germans were aiding and abetting escapees in the 1960s. Such situations involve not only legal but also humanitarian considerations. Except that there is a fundamental difference. With the intra-German escape operations, every GDR citizen who made it over the border to West Germany immediately and automatically was given all the rights enjoyed by citizens of the Federal Republic. Granted, there was an obligatory admission procedure for 'refugees from the Zone', as they were then called. Like refugees from Syria, Afghanistan, and Ethiopia today, they were put into reception camps (at that time in Berlin-Marienfelde or near Giessen in western Germany). Identity and background checks were made on each new arrival. Ultimately though, none of the citizens who fled the GDR faced deportation. The prospects for the future of those who had escaped from East to West Germany were clearly rooted in due process.

For many years I had wanted to write the story of my activities as an escape helper. I postponed acting on that desire for a long time, not finding it all that important. But given the current refugee crisis, the fact that I had announced my intention to do so in my acceptance speech, and the urging of my children, I could no longer evade this task. Many memories resurfaced during my research. I often think of 'my' refugees. I ask for understanding and forbearance from those whom I did not succeed in bringing out of the GDR. After unification, I have never personally met or even sought contact with those whom I helped to escape. With one exception, the Nuremberg couple. Only one other person has thus far managed to find me after searching for nearly fifty years.

What, after all, is 'the price of freedom'? The payments that the relatives and friends made to Fuchs? The payments that the federal German government made to the GDR via the Protestant church? The payments to Vogel and Stange that came from the two German governments as well as from the prisoners or their families? The pardons granted by the respective heads of state: Ulbricht (East Germany) and Lübke (West Germany)? The reciprocal release of the prisoners to be exchanged? The fears and worries of their families and friends? The time spent in prison?

I think back to Hohenschönhausen without resentment. It not only taught me self-discipline, but also how optimism, calm, and equanimity under adverse conditions could help a 'wild young man' cope with imprisonment, and later, with his life. I am grateful to have experienced others, and myself, in situations of extreme danger and isolation, and to have been able to help those others – truly a mutual lesson in compassion.

Appendix 1

GERMANY AND BERLIN IN 1966

After Nazi Germany's defeat at the end of Second World War in 1945, German women selflessly cleared the rubble of destroyed buildings from the streets of the country's cities and towns, while the men vigorously started reconstructing factories. This initiative was taken under the control of the four victorious Allied powers – the United States of America, the Union of Soviet Socialist Republics, the United Kingdom, and France. They had partitioned Germany into four occupied zones. The three Western powers each administered one zone in the west; the Soviet Union, the remaining zone in the east. Berlin and Vienna were similarly divided into four units, called sectors. Austria, which had been part of Nazi Germany from 1938 to 1945, regained status as an independent state not long after the end of the war, with Vienna as its capital.

In Germany, however, strong political and ideological differences between the Soviet Union and the three western Allies led to the creation of two German states: the Federal Republic of Germany (FRG), founded on 23 May 1949, with its capital in Bonn, covering the territory of the three Western zones of occupation, and the German Democratic Republic (GDR), with its capital in East Berlin, on the territory of the eastern zone, founded on 7 October 1949. East and West Germany were increasingly separated by a complex multi-fence system equipped with automatic killing devices. People illegally crossing these barriers risked their freedom and their lives. East Germany looked to the Soviet Union for political guidance; West Germany, to the United States and NATO, the intergovernmental military alliance forged to defend against Soviet imperialism. Both blocs stationed large armies and long-range missiles in the parts of Germany under their influence. By the mid-1960s, West Germany had achieved the so-called economic miracle, benefitting from massive US financial assistance and other support. East Germany never thrived, labouring as it did under an ideologically imposed planned economy that served the elites of the Soviet Union and the GDR more than most of the citizens.

Berlin gradually devolved into two entities: West Berlin (consisting of the American, British, and French sectors) and East Berlin (the Soviet sector). With the construction of the Wall between West and East Berlin from 13 August 1961 onwards, the main, most heavily guarded, and best-known border crossing between West and East Berlin was Checkpoint Charlie.

As a political enclave inside the GDR, some 100 miles (166 kilometres) from the border of the FRG, West Berlin was geographically isolated and in need of help from the FRG and the western powers to survive. The government in Bonn invested heavily in West Berlin and lured West German academics, workers, and students to that city with tax breaks, money, and a flourishing, publicly funded cultural life of affordable theatres, concert halls, museums, and opera houses. Because the Soviet Union objected to West Germany's ambition to incorporate West Berlin into its own political system, any attempts to do so prompted Soviet threats, blockades, and military terror tactics, such as regular flights of supersonic jets across West Berlin to break the sound barrier.

The author experienced and remembers all of these developments, especially after moving to West Berlin as a student of political economics and law in the spring of 1965.

Appendix 2

FRATERNITIES IN GERMANY, AUSTRIA, AND SWITZERLAND

Inspired by the French revolution and a yearning for democracy and freedom from feudal social and political structures, fraternities in the German-speaking regions go back to the late eighteenth and early nineteenth centuries. They were organised along regional, tribal, or social lines and used Latin names like Suevia (for Swabian students), Teutonia (belonging to the German Teutonic tribe), and Guestphalia (referring to the area of Westphalia). The author's own Corps, Suevia, is Heidelberg's oldest fraternity, founded in 1810. It has an impressive list of influential members. Unlike many other fraternities, Corps Suevia respects the personal views of its mostly centre-right-oriented members, irrespective of their political allegiances or inclinations.

The major attraction of fraternities lies in their network: each member has lifelong access to all of his fraternity's members of all ages and professions.

The early (solely male) fraternities have always been lifelong associations. Their main admission ritual is the *Mensur*, a domesticated form of earlier duelling in which student members of various fraternities, exposing parts of their heads and faces to possible injury, battle against each other. The goal, however, is not to win but rather to show courage and solidarity with the other members of the combatant's fraternity, so there are neither winners nor losers. Duelling fraternities were banned by the Nazis in 1935 but were re-established in the 1950s.

All members wear the colours of their fraternity's flag on a sash worn diagonally across the chest, and on various types of caps and festive jackets donned for evenings of ceremonial drinking and singing in the fraternity's drinking hall (*Kneipe*). This is usually located in the fraternity's own villa, which provides accommodation for the student members of the fraternity and is largely financed by its senior members.

The oldest groups of fraternities are *Landsmannschaften*, *Corps*, and *Burschenschaften*. Today, many other fraternity groups exist, including denominational fraternities, and even a few female ones. Women's fraternities never conduct *Mensuren*, and many of the men's fraternities have abandoned fencing. What all German-speaking and American fraternities (and sororities) often have in common is excessive drinking.

Jewish Corps, most of which were in Vienna, no longer exist. The descendants of the Jewish members, expelled by their fraternities across Germany and Austria under pressure from the Nazi government, still await an unambiguous public apology from their respective fraternities.

Appendix 3

DOCUMENTATION

The author as a student of law at Freie Universität Berlin in 1965.

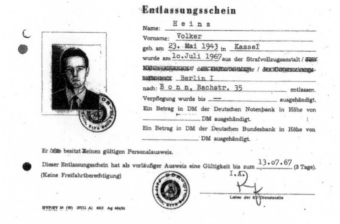

The author's certificate of discharge from prison, valid until 13 July 1967 (the actual release occurred on 11 July 1967).

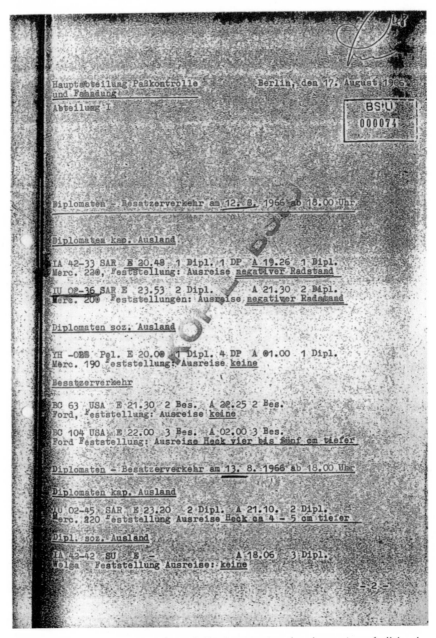

Hauptabteilung Paßkontrolle   Berlin, den 17. August 1966
und Fahndung
Abteilung I

BSU
000074

Diplomaten – Besatzerverkehr am 12. 8. 1966 ab 18.00 Uhr

Diplomaten kap. Ausland

IA 42-33 SAR E 20.48 1 Dipl. 1 DP A 19.26 1 Dipl.
Merc. 220, Feststellung: Ausreise negativer Radstand

IU 02-36 SAR E 23.53 2 Dipl.   A 21.30 2 Dipl.
Merc. 200 Feststellungen: Ausreise negativer Radstand

Diplomaten soz. Ausland

YH -028 Pol. E 20.00 1 Dipl. 4 DP A 01.00 1 Dipl.
Merc. 190 Feststellung: Ausreise keine

Besatzerverkehr

BO 63 USA E 21.30 2 Bes. A 22.25 2 Bes.
Ford, Feststellung: Ausreise keine

BO 104 USA E 22.00 3 Bes. A 02.00 3 Bes.
Ford Feststellung: Ausreise Heck vier bis fünf cm tiefer

Diplomaten – Besatzerverkehr am 13. 8. 1966 ab 18.00 Uhr

Diplomaten kap. Ausland

U 02-45 SAR E 23.20 2 Dipl. A 21.10. 2 Dipl.
Merc. 220 Feststellung Ausreise Heck ca 4 – 5 cm tiefer

Dipl. soz. Ausland

IA 42-42 SU E –   A 18.06 3 Dipl.
Wolga Feststellung Ausreise: keine

- 2 -

An excerpt from the Stasi operational file documenting the observation of all border crossings at Checkpoint Charlie by diplomats' cars with CD signs.

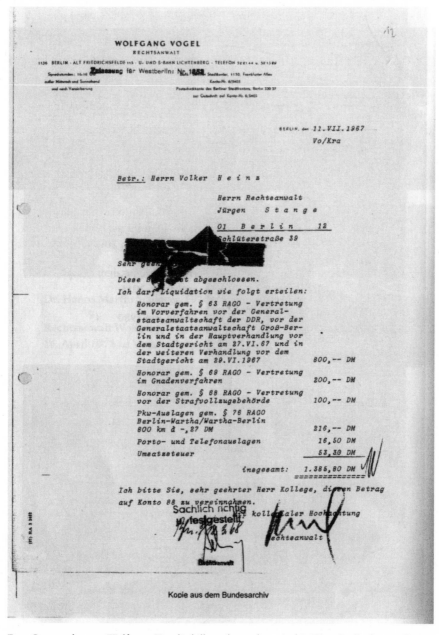

East German lawyer Wolfgang Vogel's bill to the author via his West Berlin lawyer Jürgen Stange, dated 11 July 1967, the very day of his release.

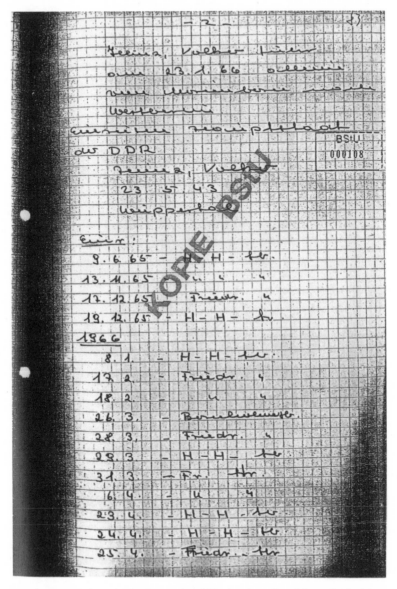

Another excerpt from the Stasi operational file showing a list of the author's visits to East Berlin in 1965 and 1966.

BIBLIOGRAPHY

Brinkschulte, Wolfgang, Gerlach, Hans Jörgen, und Thomas
Heise: Freikaufgewinnler. Die Mitverdiener im Westen.
Frankfurt am Main / Berlin 1993.

Detjen, Marion: Ein Loch in der Mauer. *Die Geschichte der
Fluchthilfe im geteilten Deutschland 1961–1989*. Müchen 2005.

Eisenfeld, Bernd: Freikauf politischer Häftlinge. In: Repression
und Haft in der DDR-Diktatur. Hrsg. von Gunter Buchstab.
Sankt Augustin 2005.

Erler, Peter, und Hubertus Knaube: *Der verbotene Stadtteil. Stasi-
Sperr-bezirk Berlin-Hohenschönhausen*. Berlin 2012.

Erler, Peter, and Hubertus Knaube: *The Prohibited District: The
Stasi Restricted Area Berlin Hohenschönhausen*. Jaron Verlag
GmbH 2008.

Hachmeister, Lutz: *Schleyer. Fine deutsche Geschichte*. Muchen
2004.

Hailstone, Allan: *Berlin in the Cold War: 1959–1966*. Amberley
Books, Stroud 2017.

Hammer, Elke-Ursel (Bearbeiterin): Dokumente zur Deutschlandpolitik. 'Besondere Bemühungen' der Bundesrepublik, Band 1: 1962 bis 1969. Häftlingsfreikauf, Familienzusammenführung, Agentenaustausch. Munchen 2012.

Keussler, Klaus-M. von, und Peter Schulenburg: *Fluchthelfer. Die Gruppe um Wolfgang Fuchs*. Berlin 2011.

Koch, Alexander: Menschen gegen Waren. Der Freikauf politischer Häftlinge aus der DDR. Darmstadt, Univ.-Magisterarbeit, 2006.

Lindheim, Thomas von: *Bezahlte Freiheit. Der Haftlingsfreikauf zwischen beiden deutchen Staaten*. Baden-Baden 2001.

Martin, Elisabeth: '*Ich habe mich nur an das geltende Recht gehalten*'. *Herkunft, Arbeitsweise und Mentalität der Warter und Vernehmer der Stasi-Untersuchungschaftanstalt in Berlin-Hohenschonhausen*. Baden-Baden 2014.

Maser, Peter: Evangelische Kirchen und Freikauf. In: Repressionen und Haft in der SED-Diktatur. Hrsg. von Günter Buchstab. Sankt Augustin 2005.

Spohr, Julia: *In Haft bei der Staatssicherheit. Das Untersuchungsgefangnis Berlin-Hohenschönhausen 1951–1989*. Göttingen 2015.

Verein der Alten Herren der Suevia zu Heidelberge e.V.: Beiträge zur Geschichte des Corps Suevia zu Heidelberg und zur Zeitgeschichte aus der Feder Heidelberger Schwaben. Zum 200. Stiftungsfest im Jar 2010. Heidelberg 2010.

Völkel, Claudia: Die besonderen Bemühungen der Bundesregierung um Haftentlassung und Üpersiedlung aus der DDR. Aus der Überlieferung des Bundesministeriums fur

innerdeutsche Beziehungen (B137) In: Mitteilungen aus dem
Bundesarchiv. 16.2008, I., S. 38–52.

Wedel, Reymar von: *Als Anwalt zwischen Ost und West. Prozesse
– Gefangene Aktionen*. Berlin 2005.

Whitney, Craig R.: *Advocatus Diaboli. Wolfgang Vogel – Anwalt
zwischen Ost und West*. Berlin 1993.

Whitney, Craig R.: *Spy Trader: Germany's Devil's Advocate & the
Darkest Secrets of the Cold War*. Times Books, Random House,
1993.

Whitney, Craig R.: Wie alles anfing ... In: DIE ZEIT, Nr. 48, 6
August 1993.

Winters, Peter Jochen: Erilicher Makler zwischen den Fronten.
Zum Tod von Wolfgang Vogel (1925–2008). In: Deutschland-
Archiv 41.2008,5, S.75–778.

Wölbern, Jan Philipp: Die Entstehung des 'Häftlingsfreikaufs' aus
der DDR. 1962–1964. In: Deutschland-Archiv 41.2008,5. S.
856–866.

Wölbern, Jan Philipp: Der Freikauf politischer Häftlinge aus
der DDR von 1962 63 bis 1990. In: Potsdamer Bulletin für
Zeithistorische Studien. 43 44.2008, S. 18–21.

Wedel, Reymar von (Hg.): Wolfgan Vogel. Eine Festgabe.
Realisiert durch das Institut für vergleichende Staat-Kirche-
Forchung. Mit Beitragen von Klaus Bolling. Berlin 2005.

PICTURE CREDITS

With grateful thanks to Allan Hailstone, author of *Berlin in the Cold War, 1959 to 1966*: Plate 1, above; plates 2, 3 and 4.

Peter Vorlicek: Plates 7 and 8.

USAMHI: Plate 1, below.

All other images are from the private archive of the author.

GLOSSARY

CDU (Christliche Demokratische Union Deutschlands) Christian Democratic Union of Germany, the name of a major interdenominational (both Protestant and Catholic) political party founded in 1945 and based on views representing the intermediate and right-of-centre segment of Germany's political and economic spectrum. The party has served in the government of the Federal of Germany for most of the period since that state's creation.

CIA (Central Intelligence Agency) The foreign intelligence service of the United States of America.

COMECON (Council for Mutual Economic Assistance) A Soviet-led, primarily Eastern-Bloc international organisation created in 1949 in response to the formation in western Europe of the Organization for European Economic Cooperation (OEEC, 1948, the forerunner of the Organization for Economic Cooperation and Development, OECD).

CSU (Christlich-Soziale Union in Bavaria) Christian Social Union in Bavaria. A German conservative Christian political party, founded in 1946, whose candidates run for office only in the Free State of Bavaria. At the federal level the CSU and its larger sister party, the Christian Democratic Union (CDU) constitute a common faction referred to as the CDU/CSU and have served with CDU in the government of the Federal Republic of Germany since 1949.

Economic miracle The period of West Germany's rapid post-war economic recovery and reconstruction from 1950 to about 1965.

FDP (Freie Demokratische Partei) Free Democratic Party of Germany. A traditionally centre-right political party founded in West Germany in 1948 with antecedents in progressive and national liberal parties of the mid-nineteenth century. It was the junior coalition partner of the CDU/CSU (1949–1956, 1961–1966, 1982–1998, and 2009–2013) and the Social Democratic Party of Germany (1969–1982).

Frankfurter Allgemeine Zeitung (FAZ) A widely respected daily newspaper with wide circulation in the Federal Republic of Germany.

FRG (Bundesrepublik Deutschland, BRD) Federal Republic of Germany (West Germany). The abbreviation used to refer to the West German state and its territory as of October 1949.

GDR (Deutsche Demokratische Republik) German Democratic Republic (East Germany). The abbreviation frequently used to refer to the East German state and its territory as of October 1949.

KGB (Committee for State Security, 1954–1991) The main domestic and foreign intelligence service of the Soviet Union.

NVA (Nationale Volksarmee) National People's Army, the armed forces of the German Democratic Republic.

Ostpolitik (Eastern policy) As initiated in 1969 in the Federal Republic of Germany by Willy Brandt as foreign minister and then chancellor, the policy of normalising relations and practising openness toward the East within the overall context of East-West détente

Palatinate Short for Rhineland-Palatinate, a federal state in the southwest of the Federal Republic of Germany.

S-Bahn (Stadtbahn) A mostly elevated rapid transit railway system serving Berlin and its environs.

SED (Sozialistische Einheitspartei Deutschland) Socialist Unity Party of Germany. East Germany's ruling political party, formed in 1946 through the forced unification of the Communist Party of Germany and the Social Democratic Party in the Soviet Zone of Occupation in Germany. It was modelled on the Soviet Union's Communist Party and ruled the German Democratic Republic until 1990.

SPD (Sozialdemokratische Partei Deutschlands) Social Democratic Party of Germany. A political party originally founded as a Marxist party in 1875 but with roots harking back to 1863. It has represented basically centrist and left-of-centre persuasions of Germany's electorate since 1959, when it renounced its commitment to socialism, voiced support for the market economy and favoured the NATO alliance. The SPD has participated in various West German coalition governments (1966–1982, 1998–2009, 2013–2018).

SS (Schutzstaffel) An elite, racially selected organisation that eventually assumed control of police functions and responsibility for the administration and operation of the concentration and extermination camps under the National Socialist regime in Germany (1933–1945).

Stasi (Staatssicherheit) The German Democratic Republic's State Security Service and the people officially working for it.

StEG (Strafrechtsergänzungsgesetz) East Germany's Penal Amendment Act, on which the arrest warrant issued against V. G. Heinz was based.

USSR (Union of the Soviet Socialist Republics, USSR Commonly also called the Soviet Union or Russia). A country established in December 1922 with the union of Russia and various other soviet republics, including Belorussia and the Ukraine.

KEY LOCATIONS AND PEOPLE

Adenauer, Konrad (1876–1967) The first chancellor of the Federal Republic of Germany (1949–1963), simultaneously also foreign secretary (1951–1955). He was a former mayor of Cologne (1917–1933, 1945), a founder of the Christian Democratic Union of Germany (1945), and that party's chairman (1950–1966). He was an anti-communist who favoured Germany's integration into the community of Western states, membership in the North Atlantic Treaty Organisation (NATO), a market-based liberal democracy, alliance with the United States, and restoration of Germany as a player in world politics.

Baden (adj. Badenese) A historical German territory constituting part of the southwestern federal state (*Land*) of Baden-Württemberg in the Federal Republic of Germany.

Brandt, Willy (1913–1992) German Social Democrat, SPD party chairman (1964–1987), Governing Mayor of West Berlin (1957–1966), foreign minister and vice chancellor (1966–1969), and chancellor (1969–1974) of the Federal Republic of Germany. As leader of an SPD-FDP coalition government, he favoured renunciation of the Hallstein Doctrine, improvement of relations with East Germany and other Eastern Bloc communist countries (*Ostpolitik*), and support for policies of the United States.

Dahlem Dorf A northern part of West Berlin's district of Zehlendorf, where the Free University was located.

Kiesinger, Kurt Georg (1904–1988) Third chancellor of the Federal Republic of Germany (1966–1969) and the first one to lead a grand coalition (CDU/CSU/SPD). He had been a Nazi party member (1933 to 1945) and eventually became the German foreign ministry's deputy broadcasting director. After World War II, he served in the lower house of West Germany's parliament (1949–1959, 1969–1980) and as Baden-Württemberg's CDU minister president (1958–1966).

Kohl, Helmut (1930–2017) The sixth and longest-serving chancellor of the Federal Republic of Germany (1982–1998), heading a coalition consisting of the CDU, CSU, and FDP. He helped bring about the unification of Germany, a goal realized with the fall of the Berlin Wall in November 1989 and the accession of the German Democratic Republic to the Federal Republic of Germany in October 1990. He is also seen as having been a key driver of European integration, which led to the creation of the European Union and introduction of the common European currency, the Euro.

Krautwig, Carl (1904–1981) A German civil servant and lawyer who served in governmental posts of the Federal Republic of Germany from 1943 to 1969, including that of Undersecretary in the Ministry for All-German Affairs (1964–1968).

Kunst, Hermann (1907–1999) Lutheran bishop and from 1950 to 1977 the first authorised representative of the Council of the Evangelical Church in Germany (EKD) to the West German federal government. He approved the use of the Protestant Church's financial network to transfer West German government payments to the German Democratic Republic for the release of political prisoners held in East Germany.

Lehrter Bahnhof From 1961 to 1990, the first West Berlin elevated rapid-transit railway (S-Bahn) station reached by westbound trains leaving East Berlin. Completely rebuilt and vastly expanded after 2000, the station is now called Hauptbahnhof (Central Railway Station).

Marienborn (Checkpoint Alpha) The checkpoint on the East German side of the border crossed by the autobahn and railroad linking Berlin and Hanover.

Memorial Church (Emperor William Memorial Church) A ruin preserved as an anti-war memorial in the centre of former West Berlin.

George, Heinrich (1893–1946) German film and stage star whose roles in major National Socialist propaganda movies and whose public addresses and appearances supporting the regime from 1933 through 1945 led to his arrest by Soviet military authorities after the Second World War.

Helmstedt (Checkpoint Alpha) The checkpoint on the West German side of the border crossed by the autobahn and railroad linking Berlin and Hanover.

Honecker, Erich (1912–1994) A ranking official of East Germany's governing political party and the person who had been in charge of building the Berlin Wall in 1961. He ultimately became the leader of the German Democratic Republic from 1971 to October 1989.

Rehlinger, Ludwig A. (1927–) A West German lawyer and ministerial official in the Federal Republic's Ministry for All-German Affairs (1958–1969), through which the release or exchange of political prisoners between East and West Germany was negotiated.

Strauss, Franz Josef (1915–1988) Controversial Bavarian anti-communist leader and leader of the Christian Social Union party (1961–1988). The many public posts he held during his long political career included that of national defence minister (1956–1962), national finance minister (1966–1969), and minister president of Bavaria (1978–1988).

Streit, Joseph The Prosecutor-General of the German Democratic Republic, 1962–1986. He was Wolfgang Vogel's chief contact within the State Security Service.

Tenhumberg, Heinrich (1915–1979) Roman Catholic prelate, Auxiliary Bishop (*Weihbischof*) in Münster (1958–1969), and Bishop of Mainz (1969–1979). From 1966 to 1969, he headed the Catholic Office in Bonn – the representation of the German bishops to the Bundstag (West Germany's lower house of parliament) and the West German federal government.

Zehlendorf A southwestern district of West Berlin.

MAPS

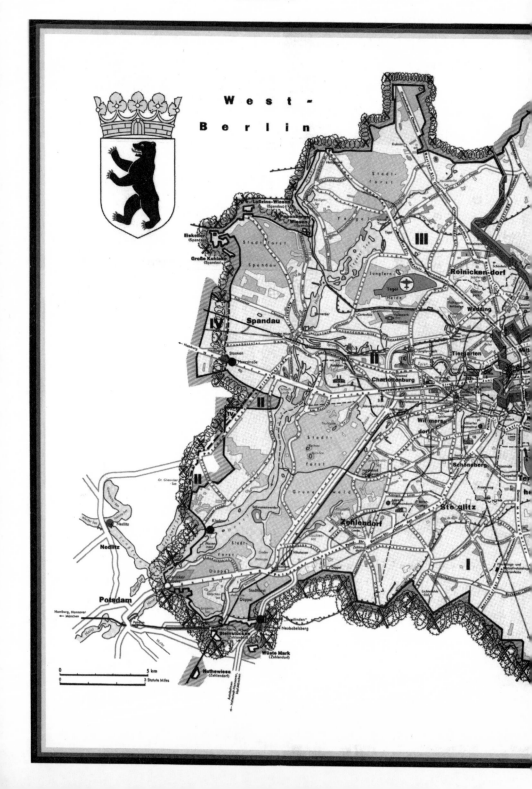

Berlin, divided into East Berlin and West Berlin, with West Berlin encircled by the Berlin wall both towards East Berlin and the German Democratic Republic.

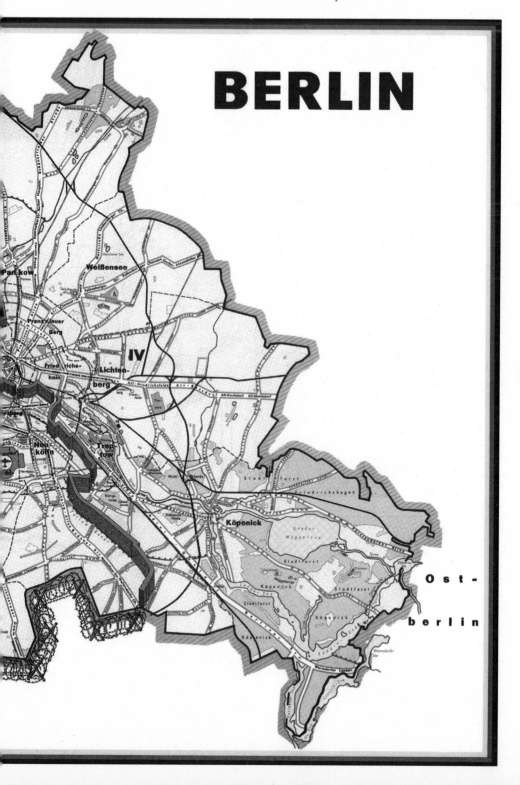

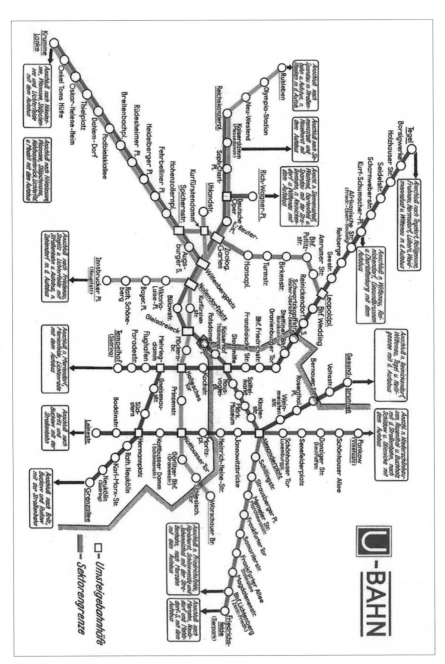

The Berlin underground network. Where the Berlin wall interrupts the lines, the journey either ended at the wall or crossed the East Berlin section without halting at the East Berlin stops. The same is true for the S-Bahn, opposite.

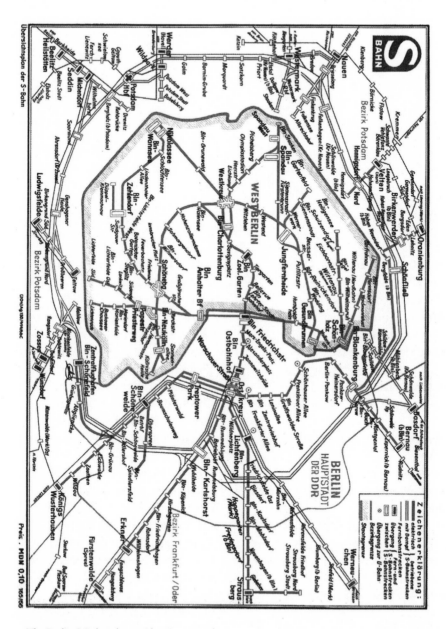

The Berlin S-Bahn, the rapid train network.

INDEX